Surrealism, Insanity, and Poetry

Surrealism, Insanity, and Poetry

J. H. Matthews

SYRACUSE UNIVERSITY PRESS 1982

Copyright © 1982 by
SYRACUSE UNIVERSITY PRESS
SYRACUSE, NEW YORK 13210

First Edition

Warmest thanks to Karol Baron for the confidence he has shown
in contributing illustrations to this volume.

Library of Congress Cataloging in Publication Data

Matthews, J. H.
 Surrealism, insanity, and poetry.

 Includes bibliographical references and index.
 1. Surrealism (Literature) 2. Literature and
mental illness. 3. Poetry. I. Title.
PN56.S87M3   809'.91   82-3165
ISBN 0-8156-2273-2   AACR2

Manufactured in the United States of America

To
Henri Peyre,
with gratitude

J. H. Matthews is a member of the committee appointed by the French government's Centre National de la Recherche scientifique to establish a center in Paris for documenting world-wide surrealism. He is American correspondent for *Edda* and *Gradiva* (Brussels), *Phases* (Paris), and *Sud* (Marseilles), magazines devoted to vanguard poetry and art. In 1977 the University of Wales conferred upon him its D.Litt., in recognition of his work on surrealism.

Born in Swansea, Wales, J. H. Matthews has been Professor of French at Syracuse University and editor of *Symposium: A Quarterly Journal in Modern Foreign Literatures* since 1965. He has edited a selection of stories by Guy de Maupassant (1959) as well as two special issues of *La Revue des Lettres Modernes*, and is the author of *Les deux Zola* (1957) and *The Inner Dream: Céline as Novelist* (1978) and numerous articles on nineteenth- and twentieth-century French literature.

His interest in surrealism has led him to write also *Péret's Score/Vingt Poèmes de Benjamin Péret* (1965); *An Introduction to Surrealism* (1965); *An Anthology of French Surrealist Poetry* (1966); *Surrealism and the Novel* (1966); *André Breton* (1967); *Surrealist Poetry in France* (1969); *Surrealism and Film* (1971); *Theatre in Dada and Surrealism* (1974); *Benjamin Péret* (1975); and *The Custom-House of Desire: A Half-Century of Surrealist Short Stories* (1975). He is also the author of *Toward the Poetics of Surrealism* (1976); *Le théâtre de Raymond Roussel: une énigme* (1977); *The Imagery of Surrealism* (1977); and *Surrealism and American Feature Films* (1979).

Contents

Preface

O NE IMPORTANT FACT has received less attention than it deserves from historians of the surrealist movement. Prime mover of surrealist activity in France from the beginning, and its most prominent theoretician, André Breton, a former medical student, first made contact with the operation of the unbalanced mind and came under its fascination at a most critical moment in his intellectual life, at a time when the poet in him was plagued by self-doubt.

During a period coinciding with his years of military service in the First World War Breton felt acute dissatisfaction with poetry, as defined by his prewar models, the French Symbolists. At the same time, he experienced profound disaffection for the poetic methods sanctioned by Symbolism and promoted in its name. Thus day-to-day conditions of service in military hospitals introduced him to aspects of psychiatry and neurology inaccessible to a layman, during a period of distressing hesitancy, while he felt tempted either to abandon altogether his cherished ambition to be a poet or else to investigate a new, more rewarding approach to poetic expression. In order to be truly vital, the latter would have to promise renewed faith in poetic action and hence revalidation of his poetic vocation.

The major concern of those young men with whom Breton discovered he had much in common at the end of the war is clear. They aimed to free themselves from a longstanding poetic tradition in which they had ceased to have any confidence. As, of necessity, they all sought a new direction, some of them reflected on lessons to be learned from, among other people, individuals who spoke, wrote, and painted under impetus from forces over which reason was obviously powerless to exert

regulatory influence. They continued to do this after the collapse of
Dada (to which almost all of them had rallied for a time), when the
surrealist movement had been formally launched with the publication of
Breton's *Manifeste du surréalisme* in 1924. By then, however, it could
not be a matter of envying the insane, of regarding mental instability as
the principal source of salvation for the contemporary poet, the best
alternative to submission to the Symbolist aesthetic. Already, among
available alternative methods, the techniques of verbal and pictorial
automatism appeared to offer a way out of Symbolism and even beyond
the impasse of Dada iconoclasm. By the mid-twenties, therefore, no
participant in surrealism needed to feel compelled to look upon insanity
as a state so desirable that someone denied access to it must inevitably
surrender in despair all hope of attaining the status of poet.

These preliminary remarks do not rest on their author's fond hope
to persuade readers that he is presenting anything new to those knowing
even very little about the background of surrealism's reaction against
and evolution beyond the poetic criteria inherited from the nineteenth
century in France. Stressing broad tendencies at the expense of individual contributions to which the surrealists are particularly sensitive—by
Baudelaire, Lautréamont, Nerval, and Rimbaud, notably, in the nineteenth century; by Apollinaire and Vaché in the twentieth—they have a
simple but essential function. They are meant to delimit the scope and
indicate the orientation of the pages that follow. Their purpose, in fact,
is to introduce a warning.

Anyone who anticipates finding below a close or even sketchy
analysis of features marking surrealist poetry that actually derive from a
condition of mental imbalance can save himself time and frustration. He
has only to note one thing before reading any farther.

This study of surrealism, insanity, and poetry does not claim or
even aspire to deal from the clinician's point of view with aspects of
surrealist poetic expression that may be properly said to reflect madness, mental disability, or emotional disorder. Its title places three elements on an equal footing, but gives precedence to surrealism. Judgment of two of them in light of the third being implied, it is fair to
indicate the following. It is surrealism and not insanity that provides the
point of reference, the pivot of the whole essay. In short, the purpose
here is to consider the relationship that, for its own ends, surrealism
establishes between insanity and poetry.

It is not simply a matter of pointing to coincidences that may seem
odd, even though there are enough of these to hold passing curiosity.
The most interesting by far is the presence (ahead of announcements for

art exhibits and for Breton's book on surrealism and painting) of two halfpage advertisements at the end of the eleventh number of *La Révolution surréaliste*. The lower one is for *transition*, modestly identified as "monthly magazine presenting the modern spirit of various continents in the English-speaking world." The other tells soberly of a professional quarterly bearing the unambiguous title *Archivio Generale di Neurologia Psichiatria e Psicoanalisi*. Readers of the first French surrealist magazine will be struck by the fact that these announcements appear in the same issue as an extract from Breton's *Nadja*, a text celebrating "The Fiftieth Anniversary of Hysteria," and a highly significant experiment in antirational verbal exchange, "Le Dialogue en 1929"—all discussed in this book. Itemizing coincidences does not take us very far, though. What really counts is the surrealists' eagerness to share the benefits they ascribe to mental disturbance, enlightening in that it brings into focus assumptions and goals that have contributed directly to molding surrealist discussion of poetry, its function and mechanism.

Some readers, not necessarily all of them antagonistic to surrealism, might expect to find below tangible proof that insanity and surrealist poetry are perfectly compatible. More than this, they might anticipate finding that poetry by surrealists and madness actually share common origins or are to be considered one and the same thing. Examination of the evidence brings out something very different and a good deal more informative.

True, exploration of representative documents—conducted on the level of poetic theory and beyond—uncovers in many surrealists an enduring preoccupation with and curiosity about insanity, regarded by all of them as a remarkably fruitful source of creative inspiration, and therefore as an admirable condition. More revealing still is the light it sheds on their meditation upon the theme of poetic inspiration, its roots, and communicable forms, in the medium of painting as well as of writing. Hence attention to published surrealist commentary on the insane and their art makes possible isolation of certain durable values that have remained distinctly characteristic of surrealists in France. The criteria set by these values illuminate the surrealist concept of poetry, what it really is and serves to accomplish, and by what means. And so the surrealists' idea of poetry is clarified, when we consider the reasons underlying and nourishing their admiration for those who, in the realm of artistic creation, have found liberation through insanity.

No less enlightening, on the broad base of surrealist poetics, are the motives governing the surrealists' behavior with respect to insane art, once they have reached a certain stage in their analysis of the goals and techniques of poetry. One cannot probe those motives without observing their effect—general disinclination among surrealists to press beyond a given point, refusal to attempt knowingly to cross the boundary separating the sane from the insane.

Surrealism does not equate poetry with madness. Nor—so long as we wish to see it for what it really is—does it authorize us to simplify the evidence and to conclude, as a result, that surrealist poetry belongs rightfully with the products of insanity. Hence the surrealists' experiments aimed at prospecting the irrational are particularly revealing of their attitude toward poetry and of the conduct it imposes on surrealist poets intent upon retaining and using faculties that the mad patently have lost.

Painting is a wager, announced André Masson in the course of a lecture written while he was still affiliated with surrealism. If this is so, then, on the wider scale of creative activity among surrealists, poetry may be regarded beyond a doubt as a game, no less serious in import for being fun to play. This is why, having begun by concentrating on hysteria and hallucination, the present study leads not to proof of insanity but to instances of its poetic simulation, to examples of game playing as a poetic mode instead of to evidence suggesting that this surrealist poet or that has fallen victim to mental decline. The plan followed here reflects, therefore, an attempt to understand a little better how surrealists conceive of poetry. It follows from a desire to retrace their exploration of man's capacity to experience poetry and to communicate with others on the poetic plane.

Tully, New York   JHM
January 1982

PART ONE

1

Surrealism and Psychosis

I T IS IMPOSSIBLE to deduce a thoroughly consistent pattern of response to surrealism among practitioners of psychiatry. As a group,
the latter appear unable to make up their minds whether to annex
surrealism, claiming it to be a respectable outgrowth of their own inter-
ests and research, whether to be reserved or skeptical in their response
to it, or whether simply to scoff at André Breton and those associated
with him.

At one extreme, sufficiently curious about surrealism's relations
with psychiatry to assemble a special section on that topic in *L'Evolution
psychiatrique*, Dr. J. Garrabé inclines to throw caution to the wind.
Commenting on a celebrated essay by Breton called "Le Message automatique," he remarks, "Use of a technical psychiatric vocabulary tends
to show that it is not a question of gratuitous research, but on the
contrary of experiments aimed at resolving scientific problems."[1] Flatter-
ing to Breton and surrealism though it may sound, such an evaluation
betrays a fundamental flaw. It attributes to the French surrealists' chief
spokesman the motive of engaging in scientific debate, without acknowledging the influence on what he wrote of a lifelong devotion to seeking
poetic discovery.

Dr. H. Ellenberger evidently would like to entice us farther still
when, in his *La Découverte de l'inconscient* (1974), he presents the
surrealist movement as "bound up, in several ways, with the history
of dynamic psychiatry." Ellenberger even intimates that, had André
Breton finished his medical studies and gone on to specialize in psychiatry, "he could very well have been able, with those new methods, to
become the founder of a new school of dynamic psychiatry." Next to this

3

commentator, Garrabé sounds restrained, presumably realizing that, following Ellenberger, we shall lose sight of essentials. All the same, Garrabé does affirm that, during the thirties, surrealism "will make an effort under its leading theoretician to do, with respect to what Régis calls in his *Précis* the artistic tendencies of sane man, what certain psychiatrists will try at the same time to do with respect to the symptoms of neurosis and psychosis: elucidate them thanks to the discoveries of psychoanalysis" (p. 16). The full import of this remark is lost on anyone who does not know that the psychiatrists to whom Garrabé alludes are those who founded the society for which *L'Evolution psychiatrique* became the official organ. Nevertheless, his meaning can escape none of his readers: "Surrealist works abolish all difference in nature between the normal and the pathological, between work of art and symptom which are envisaged in the same fashion, solely in terms of the creativity of the unconscious to which they testify." By now, therefore, he has changed the basis of discussion fundamentally, so that we face oversimplification which, however honestly come by, rests on one basic weakness. Garrabé views surrealism from outside and not from the standpoint of participants in the surrealist movement.

It is worth noting—and not only because it helps offer him some excuse—that Garrabé reports, "I have personally heard it said by several psychiatrists of the generation preceding our own, and specifically by my mentor Henri Ey and by Lucien Bonnafé, that it was through surrealism and not through medical literature that they progressively discovered psychoanalysis" (p. 23). Dr. Jean Broustra shares his colleague's high opinion of surrealism's valuable if incidental role. Broustra sees the surrealist movement as "a faithful ally" of Freudian psychoanalysis—a noteworthy factor indeed, when one considers that, as he reminds us, "Around 1925, psychoanalysis was being introduced timidly, in psychiatric circles,"[2] whereas the surrealists were already deeply involved with their dreams. Over the years, during the thirties particularly (and in France, one should add, since we are speaking of a generation of French psychiatrists), surrealists were to demonstrate the seriousness of their interest in psychiatry by opening the pages of their magazine to clinical commentators of whom the best known is Jacques Lacan. Still, this is scarcely a reason for subjecting the ambitions of surrealism to those of psychiatry, or for seeing the first as an offshoot of the second.

From another premise, Broustra proceeds more circumspectly when noting that, in Breton's 1924 *Manifeste du surréalisme*, "the claim for poetry plunges into the wake of mental illness which becomes the emblem of creative insurrection against rationalist repression linked to social power" (p. 64). Broustra rightly emphasizes that, far from being excluded, the mentally ill must be heard; "their words prompt poetic transgression of an unacceptable world." Even so, there is still some risk in following his lead, which could precipitate the deduction that madness provides surrealist poets with a model, to be imitated by any means that look promising. Jean Broustra is one psychiatrist who does not appear to have understood that, as a form of poetic protest, creativity in the insane marks but a stage along the road by which surrealists hope to attain full poetic affranchisement. Certainly, he exaggerates dangerously when referring to the surrealists as "questioners of madness as a model of liberation" (p. 65).

In his 1927 essay called *Introduction au discours sur le peu de réalité*, Breton gives prominence to surrealism's ambition to go beyond "manic-depressive psychosis" in order to reach a zone where imaginative liberty adds to the real, rather than taking from it. With fine disregard for essential detail, Broustra dates this important text from 1924. But he none the less manages to put his finger on a salient feature of surrealist theory during its early years. He astutely draws attention to the ambiguous use of the term "madness" by the surrealists. The word does not apply, he advises us to observe, to the kind of insanity that induces depression or leads to suicide, but to another form of madness altogether. Affecting the imagination, the latter nourishes poetic activity, so contributing to the rehabilitation of Sade, Lautréamont, and Nerval by those in the surrealist camp.

In his *Introduction au discours* Breton does indeed mention the "eternal challenge" of Gérard de Nerval, walking his lobster through Paris on a leash. All the same, Broustra's comments are less enlightening than the example Breton chooses to cite. To be meaningful in surrealism, the disruptive act, provocative or shocking, must be a conscious gesture, knowingly directed in protest against accepted behavioral norms. It is this, not a taste for the anecdotal, that accounts for the surrealists' curiosity about the counter-tradition of nineteenth-century French poetry, extending from the *bousingots* to the major protest mounted by Arthur Rimbaud.

We soon lose our way if we do not keep this fact well in sight. Indeed we are likely to fall into the error made by Dr. Adolfo Fernandez Zoïla who, addressing himself to the technique of surrealist automatic writing, remarks, "These processes bring to mind, as nothing else can, the hardly thinkable bet the madman makes with himself to grasp himself as another, in the difference (not always assumed) of psychopathological productions."[3] In this confused sentence one word stands out. It recurs in Fernandez Zoïla's article. Quoting Maurice Blanchot's judgment, "Automatic writing is a war machine against reflection and language,"[4] he goes on, "Bursting and subverting language are the two first orientations coming out of it: another discourse is going to emerge from the recital which . . . will bring to mind in more than one respect (and much more than has been pointed out) the processes in productions labeled psychopathological" (p. 30). The important element here is that the definition of psychopathology furnished by Fernandez Zoïla takes his argument around in a circle: "A delirious or subdelirious recital, a recital of words from the neurotic background," which he sees as sustaining "an edifice whose exteriorization reminds us in more than one respect of the trances of the phenomena of automatic writing" (p. 32).

By comparison, Garrabé seems to proceed with great prudence when he speaks of the surrealists' exploration of the unconscious through automatic writing or hypnosis: "This exploration has as its goal to demonstrate the identification of the unconscious with the conscious, the absolute continuity that links the phenomena described in the one and in the other" (p. 19). Wisely, Garrabé bids us note that "no work of interpretation is useful or desirable" in surrealism: "one must even carefully avoid it and be content to record what the unconscious dictates." All the same, even though he steers clear of any allusion to psychopathology, he comes no closer than Fernandez Zoïla to appreciating one central fact. Breton and his friends in surrealism never invoke psychopathology. Instead, they take as their model the statement of a poet, Rimbaud's "*I* is another." It is entirely consonant with their attitude that they leave it to a specialist, Salomon Resnik, to discuss in his *Personne et psychose* the psychopathological element at the core of Leonora Carrington's *En bas* (1945),[5] a record of acute psychosis by one who was its victim. They leave it to others to analyze *L'Homme-jasmin* (1970), a lucid third-person account of her passage through a succession of psychiatric hospitals by Hans Bellmer's mistress Unica Zürn, who finally committed suicide by jumping from a window. Just as significantly, while fully acknowledging the value of such texts, surrealists have never given them such importance as to invite the inference that these works represent the ultimate to which surrealist writing aspires or ought to attain.

As for the putative psychopathological sources of André Breton's inspiration, no surrealist has ever seen fit to speculate even on their existence, let alone their possible influence over the direction taken by Breton's own investigations in particular or by surrealism's in general. Jean Broustra—and not, as one might have anticipated, Adolfo Fernandez Zoïla—is alone in drawing attention to "phobic anguish," severe enough in Breton's case, he believes, to authorize reference to "neurotic phobia." Broustra traces to the latter a variety of Bretonian preoccupations, destined to become central to surrealist theory and ranging all the way from the idealization of women to the role of objective chance in human life. Presumably, he sees these as among the "magic solutions" balancing Breton's "phobic neurosis." But we look in vain for any support from among the surrealists themselves for this interpretation of evolving surrealist thought.

In the present context, it is immaterial whether surrealists happen to be too ill-informed to foresee Broustra's deductions or whether they choose to turn a blind eye to them. What really counts is that psychiatry appeals to a surrealist only within strict limits. These are imposed by ambitions that take him outside the field of clinical analysis in which, after all, he and his associates are competent to a very small degree. This explains why in *Les Vases communicants* (1932), where they are presented, and again in *L'Amour fou* (1937), Breton could claim to have "*exhausted*" the content of certain of his own dreams.

Observers who castigate Breton for naiveté seem incapable of noticing one thing. His goal was not a thoroughly exhaustive analysis such as only a trained psychiatrist would be qualified to attempt. Instead, he was well content to draw from his dream experience evidence that, entirely to his own satisfaction, backed up a theory interconnecting dreams and diurnal experience as "communicating vessels," on which his *Les Vases communicants* was built.

Setting us on the right road, recognition of the true nature of the undertaking pursued in *Les Vases communicants* spares us the basic error made by specialists in psychiatry sharing a viewpoint diametrically opposed to Garrabé's. Among these are Dr. J.-L. Armand-Laroche, who finds himself earnestly developing an hypothesis that is simply irrelevant.

Pointing, "with due deference to the surrealists," to the coherence of the unconscious, which he says "nourishes" more than it "dictates," Armand-Laroche talks about what he is pleased to term "the obscure but permanent bridges" connecting it with the conscious. He reminds us that psychiatric analysis aims at unifying the personality. Then, without a break, he continues, "Which leads us to say that, if the surrealists have had a presentiment of much and understood little, they have totally failed in their approach to psychotics."[6] Limited understanding would be detrimental indeed in any surrealist, but only if he aspired to conduct a clinical study and, moreover, if he shared at the same time the analyst's ambition to cure psychosis, or otherwise to adjust mental imbalance or at least to mitigate its effects.

Are we to conclude, though, that surrealists are disinterested in therapy for the simple reason that they are all more in need of treatment than inclined to offer it? Armand-Laroche is quick enough to dismiss this contention: "Without entering into another debate, that of the relationships of art and madness, it seems indeed necessary to answer in the negative. . . . Must we also recall that it is not enough to be psychotic to engage successfully in artistic activity?" Ironically, however, the reason he adduces to bolster his assertion is simply inapplicable: "The preoccupation of the sick is not to search for an aesthetic, for an original unconscious, but a real path, however tortuous it may be, leading them to other people." Armand-Laroche ends up only confusing the issue when he subscribes uncritically to a common misapprehension—which leads to radical distortion of the role they all ascribe to poetry in the life of man—that surrealists are committed to developing and imposing an aesthetic.

Armand-Laroche's conclusion runs, "In truth, bankruptcy occurred, even if surrealism did permit the work of Breton, Eluard, Aragon, Ernst and many others to blossom" (p. 103). Changing his image, he traces the "rout" of surrealism to the obligation felt by surrealists to "legislate, codify, give prescriptions, 'manifest.'" Although regarding this tendency as conflicting with the surrealists' goals, he sees it as unavoidable because, as he phrases it, surrealists are "mentally 'intact' men." In fact Armand-Laroche confesses to the temptation to say they are marked by "an impairing normalcy." This hypothesis is an attractive one, sounding quite authoritative. Yet it grows out of a hasty reading of surrealist theoretical pronouncements that distorts surrealist thought.

In his *Second Manifeste du surréalisme*, first published in 1929, André Breton declares, "It is up to us . . . to try to perceive more and more clearly what is being woven without man knowing it in the depths of his mind."[7] A little later in the same text we hear him insist that surrealism demands that its participants bring to the accomplishment of their mission "a new *consciousness*," that they contrive to "compensate by a self-observation that offers an exceptional value in their case for what is lacking in the presentation of so-called 'artistic' souls by men who are not artists but for the most part doctors" (p. 193).

On the one side, Armand-Laroche patronizes and then proceeds to criticize the surrealists. On the other, the latter's acknowledged leader in France casts a slur on medicine that indicates unequivocally that the distance separating surrealism from psychiatry is far greater than Garrabé realizes. Furthermore, in his second manifesto Breton goes on to indicate that Armand-Laroche's assumptions are just as misplaced as Garrabé's and give rise to equally erroneous deductions.

Surrealism, so the *Second Manifeste* informs us, is bent on "reproducing artificially that ideal moment when man, prey to a particular emotion, is suddenly gripped by that thing 'stronger than he' which propels him, under protest, into the immortal" (p. 194). In this statement, the adjective "ideal" is no more important than the adverb "artificially" and the equally significant descriptive phrase "under protest." These key words differentiate surrealism from the psychotic's experience while indicating, nevertheless, revealing parallels that usher in Breton's next comment: "If he were lucid, awake, he would come out from this tight situation in terror. The whole point is that he should not be free of it, that he should continue to speak all the time that mysterious ringing is going on: it is, in fact, where he ceases to belong to himself that he belongs to us."

Harking back to the *furor poeticus*, André Breton represents the surrealist poet as a person possessed. And yet he has already taken care to draw a dividing line between poetic possession and that by which the psychotic ceases to belong to himself. He spoke only two pages before, in a footnote drawing attention to Freud's discussion of the pathogenesis of nervous illnesses, of the inner repressions that lead us to fulfill our dreams and to compensate for the inadequacies of actual existence. When the process of transmutation fails, Breton recalled, the individual withdraws into the universe of his dreams: "in the case of sickness, he transforms them into symptoms" (p. 192). But in favorable conditions, he finds another way to move from his fancies to reality. "I mean that if he possesses *the artistic gift*, psychologically so mysterious, he can, instead of symptoms, transform his dreams into artistic creations. Thus he escapes the fate of neurosis and finds through this trick a relationship with reality."

The intent of Breton's argument is easy enough to grasp. It is perfectly clear that, in his opinion, a psychologically mysterious artistic gift will allow the surrealist to achieve sublimation—the Freudian word from which the whole footnote hangs in the second manifesto. Missing, nevertheless, is some explanation of the "trick" that will save surrealist artists from the fate of the neurotic. All the same, a clear implication of central importance underlies Breton's statement. It shows that surrealists are fully aware of engaging in what the *Second Manifeste* terms "a vertiginous descent into ourselves" and of taking "a perpetual walk right in the forbidden zone." Yet, in their continuing pursuit of poetry, they neither desire nor willingly consent to cross a dividing line between sanity and madness in which André Breton never ceased to believe, and which he wished to see maintained and respected by those investigating poetry in the name of surrealism.

2

Introduction to Psychiatry

Two sets of historical facts, seemingly unrelated, indicate how potentially confusing the surrealists' outlook on and relationship to insanity can appear, as soon as one tries examining the characteristics and manifestations of their attitude and conduct with some degree of objectivity.

1. Within two months of publication of André Breton's October 1924 surrealist manifesto a new Parisian magazine came out under the title *La Révolution surréaliste*. On August 15 of the following year the third issue of this first French surrealist review carried an "Address to the Pope," ridiculing Roman Catholicism, an "Address to the Dalai Lama," rejecting Western thought, and three open letters. All these texts presented the same features. They were printed without signature but spoke for the surrealist group as a whole. And, although no indication of this was given, all were written by the same person.

2. The French writer Antonin Artaud was institutionalized for the first time in 1915, at the age of nineteen. He was diagnosed incurably schizophrenic in 1939 and remained confined, without interruption, from 1937 until his release—in response to a public petition, and even then only in the care of a psychiatrist, Dr. Achille Delmas—two years before his death in 1948.

These facts come together in a way that promises to be misleading. All the unsigned texts published in the third number of *La Révolution surréaliste* were drafted by Artaud. What is more, the best-remembered of Artaud's open letters was addressed to the doctors in charge of insane asylums.

In 1938 a doctor at the Sainte-Anne mental hospital commented on

Artaud's condition, "Literary pretensions, maybe justified so far as delirium can serve to inspire." This medical opinion highlights a question posed early in the "Letter to Heads of Insane Asylums": "How many are you, for example, for whom someone with dementia praecox and the images to which he falls prey are anything but a hodgepodge of words?" And it gives special emphasis to the statement, "We do not allow anyone to impede the free development of a delirium, just as legitimate, just as logical as any other succession of ideas or human acts," and also to this declaration: "Without insisting on the perfect genius manifested by certain madmen, to the degree that we are qualified to judge it, we affirm the absolute legitimacy of their concept of reality, and of all acts resulting therefrom."[1] Thus the first problem facing us appears to be the following. How much weight are we to give assertions like these, when reading them with the knowledge that they were written by an individual who had already been confined to a madhouse, where he had learned to hate psychiatrists and to fear the power vested in them by society? To what extent may we take Artaud's words as representative of the position adopted by surrealists in France, rather than simply the outlook of a man speaking from a strictly personal viewpoint and for private reasons?

To appreciate how far astray some wrong inferences can lead at this stage, one has only to listen to a psychiatrist who makes no secret of his distrust of surrealism. J.-L. Armand-Laroche believes we have no more cause to blame the surrealists for "falling short of their goal" than to "glorify" Artaud for "so easily attaining it" (p. 105). He argues that Artaud had in his favor mental illness, "which placed him without effort at the heart of the problem." Then he puts forward the claim—unsupported by one shred of evidence culled from Artaudian writing—that Artaud "could allow to explode, from his fine metaphorical language derived from his morbid state, a delirium all his own that makes him unique in his surreality." The implication is quite clear: Artaud's uniqueness diminishes the value of work created by surrealists who do not share that special gift, his delirium.

Does Armand-Laroche intend to deny his own assertion that surrealism is not madness? Or does he wish rather—taking issue now with Fernandez Zoïla—to suggest that, Artaud aside, the surrealists all fall short of delirium, hence precipitating the "bankruptcy" of surrealism? Whatever the answer, his thinking is obviously confused. It leads to the hypothesis that Antonin Artaud's "literary individualism" derived from his "morbid personality" and "singularity" while yet accounting for his adhesion to the surrealist cause (p. 101).

Little is accomplished by the deduction that, because Artaud was mentally disturbed and joined their group, the first surrealists too must have lacked mental stability. And no more is achieved by the conclusion that, because Artaud and the surrealists parted company so soon, surrealism must have been undermined very quickly by the "impairing normalcy" of its faithful adherents.

When speculating on the motivation behind the "Letter to the Heads of Insane Asylums," one cannot eliminate self-interest entirely. Nor, though, can one ignore the following. In 1925 the surrealists in Paris had enough confidence in Antonin Artaud (newly appointed director of the Bureau de Recherches surréalistes, located at 15, Rue de Grenelle) to give him a free hand in putting together the third number of their magazine. Therefore it is essential to establish how much credence to give the famous open letter from *La Révolution surréaliste*, in relation to an approach to insanity that may be judged typical of surrealists as a group. Some background information will contribute to settling this basic question.

While serving as a wartime medical assistant at a military hospital in Nantes, André Breton met a future suicide, Jacques Vaché, whose behavior helped cause him to doubt the concept of poetry he had brought with him into the army. Then Breton—at the time a twenty-year-old former medical student—was ordered to report, in July of the year 1916, to the French Second Army Neuropsychiatric Center at the Hôpital du Collège in Saint-Dizier. He was to serve there until the end of November as an intern under Dr. Raoul Leroy, at a hospital where soldiers suffering from mental disorders (including cases of acute delirium) were treated upon evacuation from the front. Many years later Breton would reminisce:

> The stay I had in that place and the sustained attention I gave to what went on there have counted a great deal in my life and have had, no doubt, a decisive influence on the development of my thinking. It was there—although this was very far from being the current trend—that I was able to try out on patients the investigative procedures of psychiatry, in particular recording, with a view to their interpretation, dreams and associations of unsupervised ideas. One can already observe in passing that these dreams, these categories of associations will constitute, at the beginning, almost all the working material of surrealism. there will simply have taken place ampli-

fication of *aims* on account of which these dreams, these associations are to be collected; interpretation, yes, always, but above all *liberation* from constraints—logical, moral, and other kinds—with a view to total recuperation of the original powers of the mind.[2]

One incident in particular impressed Breton enough to cause him to allude to it no less than three times, first in 1918, then in 1926, and finally in 1952. It was an encounter he had at Saint-Dizier in 1916 with a crazed soldier who did not believe in the war and whose attitude is defined in *Entretiens* as marking the extreme point along a line linking the speculations of an idealist like Fichte and certain of Pascal's radical doubts: "It is certain that for me a certain temptation starts there that will come to light a few years later in my *Introduction au discours sur le peu de réalité*" (p. 30).

Breton's influential role in directing the surrealists' attention to certain questions and in indicating where pertinent answers might be found requires us to detail his knowledge in the field of psychiatry, as it stood almost a decade before he wrote his first surrealist manifesto.

Leroy impressed Breton considerably. He had known Jean-Martin Charcot, whose work on hysteria was to fascinate participants in the surrealist venture. At Saint-Dizier he loaned Breton books that were the basic texts for French students of psychiatry at the time: E. Régis' *Précis de psychiatrie*, both Gilbert Ballet's *Leçons de clinique médicale sur les psychoses et affections nerveuses* and his *Traité de pathologie*, Maurice de Fleury's *Introduction à la médecine de l'esprit*, Constanza Pascal's *La Démence précose*, Magnan's *Leçons sur les maladies du système nerveux*, and, presumably (it is mentioned in Breton's correspondence from Saint-Dizier), Emil Kraepelin's *Introduction à la psychiatrie clinique*.

Meanwhile, Breton had begun to take a keen interest in neurology. On January 8, 1917 he was transferred to the 22e Section d'Infirmiers militaires and, at the end of the same month, succeeded in arranging a posting to the neurological center at the Hôpital de la Pitié in Paris. There he remained until the end of September, as a "temporary intern" on Dr. Joseph Babinski's service. Babinski (whose name Breton never learned to spell correctly) is mentioned in a footnote appearing in the 1962 edition of *Nadja* (1928). The note records its author's surprise at learning that Babinski had provided technical information on circular periodic madness which forms the subject of a play much admired by Breton, P.-L. Palau's *Les Détraquées*. It carries also the following statement: "I always pride myself on the warmth he showed me—even though it led him far enough astray to predict a great future in medicine for me!—and, in my own way, I think I turned his teaching to account."[3] André Breton began doing just this, in an historically important tribute to Charcot which he drew up with Louis Aragon the year *Nadja* came out: "Le Cinquantenaire de l'hystérie" incorporated two quotations from Babinski's writings, one dating from as early as 1906, the other from 1913. Review of this evidence is in itself sufficient to persuade Garrabé that surrealism "developed from the theoretical point of view on the bases it was offered by the neuropsychiatry of the day" (p. 11).

When had Breton first met Aragon? It was in either late September or October of 1917, when they both found themselves enrolled in an army course for medical students, at the Val-de-Grâce. They were attached to the so-called *IVe fiévreux* service (a euphemism for the mentally disturbed section, "the world of madness,"[4] as Dr. Lucien Bonnafé has called it). Breton remained at Val-de-Grâce until posted out on May 16, 1918, after failing the examination that would have given him the military rank of *médecin auxiliaire*.

Although during the 1939–40 war André Breton was to serve as medical officer at the military flying school in Poitiers, he never completed his training in medicine. The reasons why he abandoned his academic studies after the First World War have never come under discussion. It is worth noting, therefore, that, if at Val-de-Grâce he was not advancing his career as a doctor, it was there—in Aragon's company —that he made a discovery of major importance for the eventual evolution of a concept of poetry formulated under the name of surrealism. For the first time André Breton read a text, known to few, that might well have distracted him from thoughts of a bourgeois professional life by contributing very significantly indeed to renewing his faith in poetry: *Les Chants de Maldoror* by one Isidore Ducasse, alias the Count of Lautréamont.

Under questioning by André Parinaud, Breton confided later, in *Entretiens*, that even Arthur Rimbaud had not affected him as much as Lautréamont. For him and several of his friends (including Philippe Soupault, with whom he coauthored the automatic texts named *Les Champs magnétiques*, in the summer of 1919), "right away there was no genius that stood up before Lautréamont's" (p. 43). At the same time, Breton implied that Ducasse's reputation among some future surrealists drew strength from preoccupations, shared by all of them, having to do with "the elucidation of the *lyrical* element in poetry." To these men lyricism meant, he explained, "that which constitutes a sort of spasmodic overstepping of controlled expression." André Breton's military service may not have made a psychiatrist of him, or even a physician. But it contributed very definitely and most positively to giving impetus and direction to his poetry and even, we see, to molding the language in which he would speak of his poetic aspirations.

During his wartime service Breton had dreamed of interning at the Salpêtrière, where Charcot had investigated hysteria. Although by the middle of 1918 there were indications that he was likely to disappoint Babinski's hopes for his future, one important fact was still clear. Before the beginning of the decade that saw surrealism launched, for someone who was not to pursue a career in medicine Breton was singularly well informed about the psychiatric nosography of the day, with regard to psychopathic states and disorders of the nervous system.

Sent back to Val-de-Grâce on September 22, 1918, André Breton remained there until September 1 of the following year—a period during which he and Soupault wrote *Les Champs magnétiques* and cofounded the magazine *Littérature* with Louis Aragon. Promoted *médecin auxiliaire* on July 1, 1919, he was demobilized September 19 after serving nineteen days at the Aviation Center in Orly. Given the vocation to which Breton willingly devoted his energies even before his military discharge, the most important feature of his initiation into psychiatry was that it coincided with a difficult moment in his life, when he was questioning very seriously his calling as a poet, his "poetic obsession," as he termed it. Letters written from Saint-Dizier to a contemporary and future associate in surrealist activity, Théodore Fraenkel, actually show Breton analyzing the complexities of his own mental state by reference to Régis and Ballet. Writing on August 15, 1916 to Guillaume Apollinaire, a poet he admired greatly, he confided, "Nothing impresses me so much as these madmen's interpretations. . . . My fate is, instinctively, to submit artists to an analogous test. From such an examination I doubt that Rimbaud will emerge unscathed (*Une Saison en enfer*) and I look with terror at what, inside myself, is going to sink with him." Breton's interest in and knowledge of psychiatry developed along with— and beyond a doubt in considerable measure as a result of—his crisis as a poet, that is, while he was asking himself what poetry is for and to what it commits the writer.

The centrally important fact that André Breton received his introduction to psychiatry at a time when he was losing trust in poets who had been his models in the prewar years directs our attention to a supposed gap in his knowledge of psychiatric theory. For whatever reason, he appears to have been unacquainted with a monograph on dementia praecox published in 1911 by Eugen Bleuler, who coined the word "schizophrenia" in order to denote functional mental disturbance. This lacuna in Breton's education was to have far-reaching consequences for his viewpoint on insanity and more especially for his attitude toward madness as a pathway to poetic discovery.

Could Breton really have remained or have been kept in ignorance of discoveries that had already superseded Kraepelin's conclusions regarding dementia praecox? Or are we to conclude that he chose to ignore them? Whatever the answer, he was to follow gladly Kraepelin's lead in reserving the term "dementia praecox" for what Bleuler had shown to be the hebephrenic types of schizophrenia. To follow Bleuler, instead, would have demanded acknowledgment of something plainly reflected in the etymology of schizophrenia: the debilitating feature of mental disturbance, which splits the personality, in conflict with the supreme surrealist ambition of unifying it. Breton and Paul Eluard could hardly have celebrated later, in their *L'Immaculée Conception* (1930), the poetic revelations of dementia praecox while agreeing wholeheartedly that schizophrenia marks the breakdown of the normal associative bonds of the human personality.

Meanwhile at Saint-Dizier, thanks to Régis' *Précis de psychiatrie* and to a book Régis wrote in conjunction with Hesnard under the title *La Psychoanalyse* (1914), Breton had been introduced to the ideas of Sigmund Freud. Freud's writings were not to begin to be translated into French until 1921 (and even then in Switzerland, not France). However, in the chapter on etiology in the fifth edition of Régis' *Précis* an extensive summary of Freud's views on psychoanalysis had appeared as early as 1914. We know that Breton was acquainted with it because he transcribed the section in one of his letters to Fraenkel.

During the twenties, influenced by John Stuart Mill and Hippolyte Taine, the leading psychiatrists—Freud, Bleuler, Janet, Jung—were all associationists. Since they looked upon the life of the mind as dominated by the automatic association of ideas, automatism was the core of scientific discussion in which Pierre Janet's *L'Automatisme psychique* (1889) and Clérambault's 1922 description of mental automatism stand out. It was not until the Blois Congrès des Aliénistes de Langue française of 1927 that the unconscious displaced automatism as the center of attention. In the circumstances—and most immediately under impetus from the stress given by Régis—it was thought association, not the interpretation of dreams, that André Breton would link first with the name of Freud. It was this same emphasis that affected the reference to Freud, in connection with surrealist automatic writing, to be found in the 1924 *Manifeste du surréalisme*:

> Taken up as I still was with Freud at that period and familiar with his methods of examination that I had had occasion to practice a little on patients during the war, I resolved to obtain from myself what we try to obtain from them, that is to say a monologue, delivered as rapidly as possible, upon which the subject's critical mind brings to bear no judgment, which is weighed down, as a result, by no reticence, and which is as exactly as possible *spoken thought*.[5]

Breton's first manifesto leaves no room for misunderstanding. The great appeal of Freud's message lay, for him, in holding out the hope and possibility of achieving *"spoken thought."* His excitement may be estimated from the fact that Leroy proposed (michievously, in Garrabé's opinion) as an eventual thesis topic for Breton's M.D. "Delirium of Interpretation in Freud."

As for the widely publicized allusion in the *Manifeste* to surrealists as "modest *recording instruments*" (p. 42), it derives from Régis' version of the Freudian method of mental association, as transcribed for Fraenkel's benefit on August 31, 1916: "The subject must note, himself, with the absolute neutrality of a witness who is an indifferent stranger or, if you wish, of a simple recording instrument, all the thoughts, whatever they may be, that pass through his mind." Among surrealists, interest in dream transcription will come only after initial experimentation with automatic writing, conducted by Breton and Soupault.

Reviewed against the surprisingly reliable knowledge of contemporary teaching in psychiatry with which Breton had equipped himself, the exploration of automatic writing he undertook in collaboration with Soupault during the summer of 1919 can be seen as having originated in genuine concern for something he later called, in *Entretiens*, "total recuperation of the original powers of the mind." In the context of Bretonian thought, this ponderous phrase is indicative of a profound conviction that traditional processes of poetic creativity are quite outdated and in urgent need of replacement. A five-year period of uncertainty—during which André Breton and his associates were more sure of what they rejected, as poets, than of what they wanted to put in its place—came to a close when, in 1924, the *Manifeste du surréalisme* gave prominence to verbal automatism as the key to poetic revelation. There is no doubt, however, that Breton was assisted in finding and using that key by his acquaintance with the methodology of contemporary psychiatric practice in France.

André Breton's thinking advanced the way it did in sharp contradiction with the argument put forward by Henri Ey. Dr. Ey is prepared to grant that insanity means *"reaching liberty,"* and that "morbid thought" is "automatic thought," free of control by what he terms "higher forms of psychic integration." Nevertheless, he declares categorically, "Madness does not produce works of art. It is not creative."[6] Others have shown themselves more sensitive to the artistic qualities of insane art— Marcel Réja in *L'Art chez les fous* (1905), Hans Prinzhorn in *Bildnerei des Geistenkranken* (1922), and Jacques Lacan in *De la Psychose paranoïaque dans ses rapports avec la personnalité* (1932), to cite only those known to Breton. No other commentator, however, has had Breton's vested interest in drawing attention to those same qualities.

A celebrated notice on the subject of *l'art brut* published by Jean Dubuffet in October 1948 spoke respectfully of works of art created by people "considered mentally ill" and confined to psychiatric wards. The same year André Breton voiced full agreement with Dubuffet's statement that the reasons why a man is "reputed to be unsuited to social life" do not have to be taken into account. Yet, important for surrealists as are the implications of the treatment meted out to the insane in society, they take second place, in Breton's mind, to the significance in resisting commonsense prejudice that he ascribes gladly to insane art and writing, "those trophies of the true 'spiritual hunt' through the great 'derangements' of the human mind."[7]

It is especially worthy of notice that Breton was not alone among the surrealists, in looking upon the products of insanity the way he did. In the spring of 1958 the Parisian surrealist magazine *Le Surréalisme, même* published in its fourth issue an essay by a nonsurrealist critic, Theodor Spoerri, describing a wardrobe decorated by Adolph Wölfli, a schizophrenic imprisoned at the age of twenty-four (his crime had been raping little girls) and institutionalized as a paranoid psychotic at the age of thirty-one. Spoerri commented, "Without being 'art,' Wölfli's drawings have also provoked the interest of artists." This evaluation prompted a collective statement in the form of an editorial footnote— supposedly written by the magazine's editor, André Breton—running as follows:

Without for all that adopting the views of Mr. Jean Dubuffet who, some time ago, contended rather amusingly that "there is no insane art, any more than there is dyspeptic art or art by people with knee trouble" (*L'Art brut préféré aux arts culturels*, 1949), we have difficulty seeing in the name of what ultra-retrograde conception of art Adolph Wölfli could not be considered one of the three or four greatest contemporary masters. While thanking Mr. Theodor Spoerri for his valuable analysis and without daring to ask him what he thinks of the Nerval of *Aurélia* or of the Van Gogh of Arles, we cannot refrain from voicing all kinds of reservations on this point.[8]

All in all, one can only falsify perspectives by suspecting that Antonin Artaud's "Letter to the Heads of Insane Asylums" did not carry the unreserved endorsement of those individuals who, by 1925, had joined the surrealist cause. True, there are a few distressing ambiguities in Artaud's text. We would welcome clarification, notably, on the role of meaningful responsibility in anyone who finds verbal images "to which he falls prey" in dementia praecox. Or at least we need to be told forthrightly if, in his condition, responsibility has become an irrelevant factor. More than this, we should know on what grounds "certain madmen" are to be treated as accredited geniuses while, by implication at all events, genius is to be denied others even though, in them too, delirium develops freely. Obviously, the whole question of degree to which surrealists are "qualified to judge" is fundamental and crucial in this area. It is all very well for André Breton to ridicule conventional criticism for being unable to deal adequately with the products of insanity. We still progress very little when he tells us, in his "L'Art des fous," that what madmen produce is sometimes *admirable*.

In the context of surrealist theory, we must conclude, neither the credibility of Artaud's remarks nor their representative value should give us pause. Our real difficulty, then, is setting limits within which surrealists can be expected to look upon insanity as artistically or poetically productive. This, indeed, is the central problem facing anybody trying to examine their attitude toward insanity. It brings us to *Nadja*.

3

Hysteria and Poetry

PUBLISHED ON MAY 25, 1928, André Breton's *Nadja* is commonly taken to be a work of fiction and so is treated as pure (or almost pure) invention. Thus the publishers of its English-language edition presented it ambiguously as "the first and perhaps best Surrealist romance ever written," adding, "The Nadja of this book is a girl, but like Bertrand Russell's definition of electricity as 'not so much a thing as a way things happen,' Nadja is not so much a person as the way she makes people behave. She has been described as a state of mind, a feeling about reality, a kind of vision, and the reader sometimes wonders whether she exists at all." Reading Breton's book as a novel, all too many people have followed this lead. They have failed therefore to take account of the contempt for fiction openly expressed in Breton's first surrealist manifesto. Apparently, they also have remained insensitive to the irony that induced the author to set down Nadja's prediction, "André? André?... You'll write a novel about me. I assure you. Don't say no" (p. 100).

Presumably, the alternative to fundamental distortion of the purpose underlying the composition of *Nadja* is too unsettling or perhaps seems too far-fetched for most readers. They would rather treat the book as a fictional experiment than acknowledge it to be a factual retelling of events in which André Breton was really involved. They prefer not to face what confronts us all in this record of incidents beginning October 4, 1926, the day Breton for the first time, and quite by chance, met a strange young woman who chose to call herself Nadja "because in Russian that's the beginning of the word hope and because it's only the beginning of it" (p. 62).

21

In a foreword supplied for the 1962 edition, Breton mentions two imperative "antiliterary" principles to which *Nadja* was submitted. One of them calls for replacing description (ridiculed as early as the 1924 *Manifeste du surréalisme*) with photographs of people, places, paintings, and things to which the text refers. The other bases the tone to be adopted on that of medical observation, and especially on neuropsychiatric observation. Yet despite these principles we hear the writer declare, "That which I hold to be the objective manifestations of my existence, more or less deliberate manifestations, is only what passes within the limits of this life from an activity whose true field of action is quite unknown to me" (pp. 7–8).

So far as he himself is concerned, Breton confides, what matters is not so much the way things are arranged as "the disposition of the mind" with respect to that way (p. 14). So we soon hear him talking of "those perpetual solicitations seeming to come from outside," to which the secret, he says, lies in ourselves (p. 16). His announced goal is, logically, to relate, in the "margin" of the account he has to give, the most striking episodes of a period in his own life *"as I can conceive it beyond its organic plan"* (p. 18), in other words, as it introduces him to a world of "sudden parallels," of "petrifying coincidences," and "reflexes taking precedence over any other mental flights" (p. 19). His attention, readers are forewarned, will be concentrated on "certain links, certain combinations of circumstances that go well beyond our understanding, and permit our return to reasoned activity only if, in most cases, we appeal to the instinct of self-preservation" (p. 20).

All these remarks deserve to be weighed carefully by the reader who does not wish to distort the import of *Nadja*. They lose their point entirely, seeming to be tokens of literary posturing, to anyone having no appreciation of the importance of André Breton's meeting with Nadja in connection with his evolving ideas on the relationship of poetry to insanity. Almost two years exactly after the appearance of his first surrealist manifesto, this admirer of Charcot and, incidentally, former associate of Babinski ("celebrated contemner of hysteria," as Broustra calls him [p. 66]) met a real-life hysteric.

Jean Broustra interprets *Nadja* as evidencing its author's neurotic and creative anguish. He looks upon the episode involving the hysterical young woman as following a period during which surrealism's main spokesman in France had "idealized" delirium as "violence necessary to the emergence of poetry" (p. 68). Exaggeration aside, this argument loses strength by forcing the facts: Breton's letters from Saint-Dizier do not minimize in the least the price paid by psychotic hospital patients for poetic revelation. The really noteworthy feature of his encounter with Nadja is that it took place outside the closed environment of medical observation which encourages and actually requires clinical detachment. Thus, soon after he laid the theoretical basis of surrealism, André Breton had occasion to see, from close up in the outside world, what kinds of difficulties impede the practical reconciliation of poetic liberation and mental alienation.

Speaking of to the statue of Etienne Dolet on the Place Maubert in Paris (photograph reproduced in his text) Breton informs us that it has always attracted him, at the same time causing him "unbearable uneasiness." Having done so, he expresses the hope that he will not be thought in need of psychiatric help, even though he says he "esteems" the psychoanalytical method. Breton believes, he insists, that psychiatry "aims at nothing less than expelling man from himself," while still not being convinced, though, that it is up to its task (p. 23).

At the end of their first meeting, in response to Breton's earnest question, "Who are you?" Nadja answers, "I am the wandering soul" (p. 69). During their third date (on October 6), this wandering soul confides that she feels sure an underground passage runs from the Palais de Justice and around the Hôtel Henri IV. "She is disturbed," we learn, "by the idea of what has happened already and will happen again" on the Place Dauphine, where she finds herself in Breton's company. "Where at the moment only the shadows of two or three couples are melting away, she seems to see a mob." Now she cries excitedly, "And what about the dead, the dead?" (p. 81). When, next, she successfully predicts that a window with red drapes will light up across the square, Breton comments, "I admit that fear takes hold of me here, just as it is beginning to take hold of Nadja" (p. 82). Meanwhile the young woman is horrified at the sight of blue wind passing through the trees. She recalls that, on one occasion in the past, at this very location she heard a voice saying, "You will die, you will die." Indeed, feeling giddy, she would have fallen, then, from her hotel window overlooking the Place Dauphine, had her lover not restrained her.

By the time Breton decides they had better leave the square, Nadja is trembling all over. She affirms that she has been in prison— but this was centuries ago. She grasps hold of a railing, convinced she and Breton must remain at this very spot. She refuses to answer his questions any more, musing upon her life while in Marie-Antoinette's entourage. As well he may, Breton feels concern. However, by the time he has managed to loosen Nadja's fingers from the railing, half an hour has elapsed. In an effort to calm her, he recites a Baudelaire poem, but it only causes her more alarm. Stopping again, this time to look over the embankment, Nadja sees a flaming hand over the water of the Seine. She exclaims, "You think I'm very sick, don't you? I'm not sick" (pp. 84–85). If Breton vouchsafes a reply, there is no sign of it in his account.

By midnight the couple are in the Tuileries gardens. There, to Breton's astonishment, when describing one of the fountains Nadja uses an image he has come across recently in a book she surely cannot have read. She has ceased to listen to him, however. She is talking to herself, now, uttering remarks he finds of uneven interest. "I am beginning to feel tired," he confides to his audience (p. 87). They stop off at a bar, but soon are obliged to leave because the pattern of a mosaic decoration has frightened Nadja. The evening is over at last.

Anyone can see that, although André Breton talks of the neuro-psychiatric detachment of his version of events, he abstains from commenting on the symptoms displayed by his female companion. In fact, *Nadja* seems to demonstrate quite eloquently "the contempt that in a general way I have for psychiatry, for its pomps and vanities and for its work" (p. 133). Even so, it is perfectly plain to readers with far less knowledge of psychiatric nosography than Breton that, from their first meeting on, Nadja is in urgent need of treatment. October 10 finds her identifying an old woman in the street as a witch. This is no mere fanciful amusement, Breton perceives: "I am scared to note that she is trembling, literally 'like a leaf'" (p. 103). All the same, it takes him quite some time to come to the following admission: "I know this *departure*, for Nadja, from a point where it is already rare, so bold, to wish to arrive, came about in contempt of everything it is customary to invoke the moment one is lost, deliberately very far from the last raft, at the expense of everything that makes up the false but almost irresistible compensation for living" (p. 111).

How much self-deception, we wonder, entered into André Breton's attitude toward Nadja; how much hypocrisy? He reports that the day after the alarming evening of October 6 he suffered from a headache that, "rightly or wrongly," he attributes to the emotion of the night before and to the "effort of attention and accommodation I had to contribute" (p. 88). Confessing now that he spends too much time observing Nadja, he frankly admits, "It is unforgivable of me to go on seeing her [and, one might add, even more reprehensible to go on kissing her] if I do not love her." In her state, he acknowledges, "she is necessarily going to need me, one way or another, all of a sudden." Why continue to meet her then? Avowing that, close to her, he feels closer to the things close to her, he offers this excuse. If he stopped seeing her, he "would not *know*." Furthermore, he would not deserve to know. Everything he has to say in his book, in other words, follows upon the question with which it opens: "*Qui suis-je?*" In pursuit of Nadja (*je suis*), Breton dedicates himself to finding out who he himself is (*qui suis-je?*)— without concern, really, for the well-being of the person he is following.

Breton's willingness to jeopardize Nadja's mental health out of devotion to his own curiosity is soon beyond doubt. After meeting her both on October 4 and on the 5th, he notes, not without a trace of smugness, "It is clear that she is at my mercy" (p. 90). In spite of this, he searches for her (by taxi) for the third day in succession, finding her, again quite by accident. Now, as he kisses her "very pretty teeth," she exclaims, "Communion takes place in silence... Communion takes place in silence," explaining afterward that his kiss has left her with the impression of something sacred, in which her teeth "stood for the host" (p. 93).

By the next day Breton is willing to confess, "I dread her disappearance more than ever" (p. 94). Indeed, only his failure to track her down prevents him from meeting her the fourth day running. He tries to catch up with her again, we notice, even though, on the third day, she spoke openly of his "power" over her, of "the ability I have to make her think and do what I want, perhaps more than I think I want." In addition, he reports, "She pleads with me, this way, to do nothing against her." Later, with unconcealed self-congratulation, he will tell us, "I know that *she* in the full force of the term came to take me for a god, to believe I *was* the sun" (p. 110)—an image hardly offset by the one he records on the next page, when remembering having appeared to her "black and cold like a man struck down at the feet of the Sphinx." Later still he will note, "Even if that was no credit to my discernment, I admit it did not seem to me extravagant, among other things, that sometimes Nadja happened to hand me a piece of paper signed 'Henri Becque' on which the latter gave her advice." The important indicator here is his subsequent admission: "If this advice was unfavorable to me, I would confine myself to replying, "It's impossible that Becque, who was an intelligent man, could have told you *that*'" (p. 136).

Breton's deliberate manipulation of the young woman is indisputable. "Some days," he says, Nadja "seemed to live off my mere presence, without giving the least attention to my words, or even, when she spoke to me of things indifferent to me or was silent, taking account in the least of my boredom" (p. 116). The first indication that his interest in her is waning comes no later than October 11. When Nadja arrives late for their date, "I expect nothing exceptional from her" (p. 103). And in fact it makes him "impatient" to see her reading the menus outside restaurants and juggling with the names of certain dishes: "I am bored," he tells us flatly (p. 104). His interest is revitalized, though, on the 12th, when "her dream" takes on "a mythological character I did not yet know it had" (p. 106). None the less, although responsive to Nadja's assumption of the character of Melusina, Breton confesses to experiencing difficulty at this point in following her soliloquy, which "long silences are beginning to render untranslatable for me." Within a few more pages he is asking pointedly, "Can it be that this headlong pursuit is coming to an end?" (p. 109).

How much longer their relationship continues is not at all clear. But at last the moment arrives when Breton writes laconically, "They came, a few months ago, to inform me that Nadja was insane." Following certain "eccentricities in which, it seems, she had indulged in the hallways of her hotel," she had had to be committed to the Vaucluse asylum (p. 127). So far as we know, she never left there again.

Only after alluding to Nadja's fate does Breton report on an episode one would have thought memorable enough to find a place in the body of his account (undertaken, we know, only after Nadja's incarceration) instead of being relegated, the way it is, to a footnote in the concluding section of his book. His reason for not mentioning it earlier, he gives us to understand, is that he did not realize, before, how much Nadja's attitude toward him derived from "the application of a more or less conscious principle of total subversion" (p. 143), of which he now proceeds to cite just one example.

As he was driving her back from Versailles to Paris one evening, Nadja's foot began to press down on the accelerator, her hands meanwhile seeking to cover his eyes, "in the oblivion that an endless kiss brings." Breton gives it as his opinion that she "wanted us to exist no more, doubtless forever, except for one another," while the car headed toward the trees lining the roadway. "What a test for love, indeed."[1] His very next sentence bears witness to Breton's realization that, before this incident occurred, his encounter with Nadja already had ceased to have merely the character of *"provocation,"* mentioned earlier on: "Needless to say I did not accede to that wish." Why should there be any need for him to insist he had not let his passenger entice him to commit suicide? Is there more to be noted in all this than the very existence of Breton's book suffices to make perfectly explicit?

We can see plainly that André Breton has no apology to bring forward at this stage. However, retrospectively he does muster an explanation of sorts. He duly stresses his gratitude to Nadja for having revealed to him, "in a terribly striking fashion, what a common recognition of love would have committed us to at that moment" (p. 144). At the same time, though, he takes particular care to remind his audience, "You know where I stood, where so far as I know I have almost always stood with Nadja" (pp. 143–44). Earlier, indeed, he declared, without the disturbing indecisiveness introduced by the word "almost" into the sentence we have just read, "Everything that makes one able to live someone else's life, without ever desiring to obtain from that person more than he or she is giving . . . on my side did not exist either, had never existed: that was only too sure. It could not be otherwise, considering the world that was Nadja's." This then is Breton's defense, set forth over several pages of his text: "From the very first day, I have taken Nadja for a free genie, something like those spirits of the air that certain magical practices permit one to attach momentarily to oneself but there can be no question of subjugating" (p. 110). He appears to be speaking with quite refreshing honesty when he concedes, "I was perhaps not up to what she proposed" (p. 127).

How valid is Breton's explanation, all the same? The absence of passionate involvement surely did contribute to dictating his conduct in the car. Even so, no evidence coming down to us from situations involving other women (including Suzanne Musard who engaged his attention while he was writing *Nadja*, where he speaks of his love for her, before addressing her as X in *Les Vases communicants* of 1932) suggests that, when he really was in love, or when he thought himself to be, André Breton ever was seriously tempted to make a suicide pact of the kind popularized by the nineteenth-century romantics. It is evident that drawing a line where good sense recommended was, for him, part of the privilege of belonging to the *"so very prehensile tail"* of romanticism, as surrealists are defined in his *Second Manifeste du surréalisme* (p. 184).

Breton voices his indebtedness to Nadja for having made him understand "almost the necessity" of the temptation she extended. He goes further, linking it with "an extreme power to challenge," the sign by which, in his estimation, "certain very rare beings" will always recognize one another. Obviously, following this line of thought brings him to his next assertion: "Ideally at least I often find myself again, blindfolded, at the wheel of that crazy car," as well as to the declaration with which he closes his footnote in *Nadja*: "In matters of love, it could be for me, in the requisite conditions, only a matter of resuming that night ride" (p. 144). We are reminded of the narrator of Camus's *La Chute* concluding his confession (after speculating about being given, tardily, a chance to redeem himself) with the damning comment, "But let's not worry about it! It's too late, now, it will always be too late, luckily!"

The parallel with a character from Camus's fictional universe may appear not only unfavorable to André Breton but positively unjust. Yet one fact stands out as unquestionable. Only in retrospect, while reliving the scene in the safety of his imagination, "ideally," does surrealism's leading spokesman see himself responding to Nadja's urgent invitation to self-destruction. So long as he was in her presence, the motive behind his conduct vis-à-vis the temptress was caution. The important element here is the following, then: however much not being in love may have assisted Breton in maintaining his distance, what impresses us in the end is his demonstration of the virtue of prudence—to say nothing of his firm conviction, at the time of placing the whole incident on record ("Needless to say . . ."), that he was absolutely right in being wary and dedicated to self-preservation. Thus his behavior in the speeding car is exemplary of his attitude, not only toward a woman called Nadja, but toward the group of people to whom her incarceration in a mental hospital confirmed that society believed she belonged.

Unintentionally, André Breton found himself summarizing in a footnote to *Nadja* the ambiguities and inner contradictions characterizing his posture before the spectacle of insanity. He brought into focus, coincidentally, the question of surrealism's relations with insane art, understood in the widest sense of the term.

Looking back to the first surrealist manifesto, we read, "I could spend my whole life inciting the mad to confide in me. Those are people of scrupulous honesty, whose innocence is equalled only by my own" (p. 18). *Nadja*, though, lets us see Breton provoking a person of doubtful mental stability not only to confide in him, but also to act in ways that subsequently leave him feeling guilty of having accelerated her decline into madness. There is no doubt that he was grossly selfish in his dealings with Nadja. When in his book he speaks of her "value" (p. 126), he implies without hesitation the value he himself attributes to her. As for extenuating circumstances that excuse his conduct, we become aware of these only when he points out, "I had, for quite a long time, ceased to have an understanding with Nadja. To tell the truth, perhaps we never had an understanding, at least about how to look upon the simple things of existence. She had chosen once and for all not to take account of them, . . . to make no difference between the otiose remarks she happened to make and the others that mattered so much to me" (p. 125).

In other circumstances, the irony of Breton's position would be amusing. This was not only a man whose acquaintance with psychic disorders should have revealed to him at once with what manner of person he was dealing. He was also a man whose first surrealist manifesto shows him to have been keenly aware that dialogue brings into confrontation two monologues more or less hostile to one another, even when one of the people involved is not subject to pathological malfunction. Yet we hear him grumble because Nadja did not differentiate between those of her remarks that appealed to his imagination and those that did not. Could he really have believed Nadja was speaking for his benefit and not for her own? And on top of this, he complains that indifferentism, in her case, followed upon a decision for which he pettily holds her responsible, as though she were simply being stubbornly contrary. Breton's fundamental error, supposedly, was to assume that Nadja's conduct reflected deliberate choice, rather than irresistible compulsion.

The mysterious causes of Breton's inexplicable error of judgment remain conjectural. The most one can infer from purely textual evidence is that the effects of his eagerness to "*know*," to learn something precious from contact with Nadja, were, in the short run, indisputably pernicious. They led him to display an illogicality for which only someone rigorously trained in clinical observation would have less excuse than he. Moreover, they bred in him a temporary but still shocking callousness, for which he was soon to express regret. But oddly enough even in baring his conscience Breton betrayed a curious inconsistency.

If we are to accept without demur that André Breton really meant what he said in his 1924 manifesto, then it looks as though he ought to have felt none of the guilt put into words later, in his *Les Vases communicants*. Discussion of the insane, in the *Manifeste du surréalisme*, had led him to this statement: "But the profound detachment they evince with regard to the criticism we make of them, even with regard to the various punishments inflicted upon them, lets us suppose that they derive great comfort from their imagination, that they enjoy their delirium enough to bear the fact that it is valid only for themselves" (p. 17). Should this indeed be the case, ought not Breton to have been congratulating himself, in due course, when all the evidence was in, for having pushed his young companion of a few weeks over the brink, instead of blaming himself for possibly having done so?

Thinking he may have played a decisive role in causing Nadja's state to deteriorate implies, on Breton's part, giving at the very least some credence to Babinski's view that hysteria is "a pathological state manifesting itself in disturbances that it is possible to reproduce by suggestion, in certain subjects with perfect exactitude, and which are likely to disappear only under the influence of persuasion (counter-suggestion)." Yet in a famous tract put out in 1928—the same year as *Nadja* was published—Breton and Louis Aragon granted the validity of Babinski's definition only so far as they accepted it as "a moment in the development of hysteria." Moreover, their own definition spoke eloquently for itself:

> Hysteria is a more or less irreducible state characterized by subversion of the relationships set up between the subject and the mental world from which in practice he thinks he derives, outside any delirious system. This mental state is founded on the need for reciprocal charm, which explains the hastily accepted miracles of medical suggestion (or counter-suggestion). Hysteria is not a pathological phenomenon and can, in every respect, be considered a supreme means of expression.[2]

It is not hard to see why the surrealist ethic—which from the beginning taught that an individual may be a poet in the way he lives his life, whether he writes anything or not—imposed profound modification of Babinski's view of hysteria. Commenting in the second number of the surrealist magazine that replaced *La Révolution surréaliste* in 1930, and speaking on the subject of recent evolution in medecine so far as it touched on psychology, André Breton was to argue that it was directed mainly toward

> the increasingly abusive denunciation of what, since Bleuler, has been called autism (egocentrism), a most convenient denunciation, from the bourgeois standpoint, since it allows us to consider pathological anything in man that is not pure and simple adaptation to the external conditions of life, since it aims secretly to exhaust every case of refusal, of insubordination, of desertion that up until now did or did not appear worthy of respect (poetry, art, the passions of love, revolutionary action, etc.). Autist, today, are the surrealists (for Mr. Janet—and for Mr. Claude, no doubt).[3]

We shall have to return to look more closely at the social aspects of the surrealists' defense of the insane against psychiatrists, those guardians of social norms. For the moment, let us concentrate on "Le Cinquantenaire de l'hystérie." Its publication was occasioned by the discovery, in the archives of the Salpêtrière Hospital, of photographs of some of Charcot's patients, those he was treating as hysterics.

American surrealist Franklin Rosemont assures us that Aragon and Breton demonstrated in this short text "not only how little surrealism owed to the categories of traditional aesthetics" for the theory of creative expression it defended, but also "how far the practice of poetry—as 'restored and enlarged' by surrealism—had advanced beyond the outmoded and static framework of the clinicians."[4] But this comment prefaces an explanation that is really no more than a form of question-begging. Asking what was so appealing about hysteria to the founders of surrealism (only two of whom, as it turned out, actually signed the statement printed in La Révolution surréaliste, next to an extract from Nadja), Rosemont goes on to affirm:

> Surely its very special ardor, its tendency toward a kind of traumatic lyricism, its subtly veiled erotic undercurrent, the "excessive emotionalism" by which some dictionaries have been content to define it, and especially its automatic utilization of wildly improbable imaginary structures—all these attractions, among many others, naturally enlisted the sympathetic attention of those who, by their own means, were reclaiming the rights of the imagination and calling for "poetry made by all." Many of surrealism's first weapons—automatic writing, sleeping fits, convulsive dreams—could be found as well in the arsenal of hysteria. (pp. 4–5)

There is indeed a surface resemblance between surrealist poets and victims of hysteria. Both willingly adopt a submissive posture—the one before the subliminal message, the other before hysterical symptoms. In fact, when discussing the latter Pierre Janet coined the phrase "la belle indifférence" to characterize the patient's complacent acceptance of them. But acceptance, in this instance, stems from the patient's lack of confidence in himself. One can scarcely argue that the surrealist poet suffers from the same weakness. And hysterical symptoms are, after all, a distress signal, indicative of partial surrender. In this sense, they are profoundly different from the assertive act of poetic creation in surrealism. The best one can say is that surrealists have reason to admire the effect of hysteria, manifestations of its presence, and not hysteria itself. Indeed, the outward movement characteristic of poetic communication actually reverses the movement typical of hysteria. Thus poetic enunciation in surrealism is far distant from the obsessional rumination through which mental disturbance may declare itself. If this were not so, then Paul Eluard would have had no excuse for seeing the poet as *halluciné par excellence* while yet regarding the function of poems as to inspire, not evoke.

Interestingly, the conflicting comments maliciously drawn by Franklin Rosemont from a variety of medical sources do more than illustrate how elusive hysteria can appear to be, to the clinical mind. They indicate at the same time how subjective its definition can be. These observations, derided by Rosemont, bid us take care, as we listen to the surrealists' enthusiastic praise of a "poetic discovery" for which no objective definition imposes itself with any degree of authority.

Even if an unassailable definition were to present itself for hysteria, "that Proteus that cannot be laid hold of," as the seventeenth-century physician Thomas Sydenham called it, so providing a truly solid basis about which no one would have reason to quibble, we still should be obliged to face one question of fundamental importance. Why, given the circumstances, did Breton wonder, so pessimistically, if Nadja would not be fortunate enough to regain her sanity? Is good fortune not to be equated—by his lights—with remaining in a state of mental disorder, uncomplicated by glimmers of rationality? After all, in his essay on "L'Art des fous" he does not hesitate to advance the idea—"paradoxical only at first sight"—that "the art of those relegated to the category of the mentally ill constitutes a reservoir of moral health," precisely because it escapes "everything tending to falsify the testimony that claims our attention and belongs to the order of external influences, self-interest, success or disappointment encountered on the social plane, etc." For, according to Breton, "the mechanism of artistic creation is liberated from all impediment." In addition, "by an overwhelming dialectical effect," confinement to an institution (with its attendant "surrender of all profit, as of all vanity") is to be seen as "a guarantee of total authenticity" of a kind we face nowhere else (p. 516).

It is noteworthy that André Breton is bending the evidence a little, now. How can one speak of insane artists as giving up all profit when (so far as we know, any way) these are people for whom material profit may have no meaning any longer, but who still derive from their creative work a sense of accomplishment, providing all the reward they require? Yet this is not the central problem. What remains perplexing is that, in *Nadja*, Breton should feel it necessary to "denounce, in matters of mental health, the process of that almost fatal progress from acute to chronic" (p. 132). Does mental decline have any measurable value, except to a detached observer, when "the essential thing is that for Nadja I do not think there can be an extreme difference between the inside of an asylum and the outside" (p. 128)?

No answer to this question is formulated either in the book *Nadja* or in the tract "Le Cinquantenaire de l'hystérie." Nor, for that matter, does it come to us fifty years later, in the catalogue *Surrealism in 1978: 100th Anniversary of Hysteria*. Asking what it is (theoretically, any way) that attracts surrealists in hysteria, we learn that it is nothing less, to Aragon and Breton, than the appeal of "the greatest poetic discovery of the end of the XIXth century." In Breton's mind, in fact, hysteria has rated consistently high ever since, in a 1920 essay on Louis Bertrand's *Gaspard de la nuit*, he called it "one of the finest poetic discoveries of our period."[5] In short, "Le Cinquantenaire de l'hystérie" does no more than underscore the paradox of Breton's concern about Nadja's possible rehabilitation: curing her implies "curing" a poetic discovery.

The danger—and from the surrealist's viewpoint this word does not sound excessive—is a serious one. To see why, we have only to examine the case of Aimée, the psychopath studied in Lacan's *De la Psychose paranoïaque dans ses rapports avec la personnalité*.

After attempting to strangle a publisher who had declined to bring out her novels, Aimée was arrested for trying to stab a well-known actress. Passages from her manuscripts were published for the first time in Lacan's thesis, where they at once drew the surrealists' interest. One of the group, René Crevel (a future suicide), commented in a surrealist magazine on their "extreme interest" for the light they cast on their author's mental state, adding, "But above all, the liveliness, the grand subtle pace of her writings testify to a poetic value intransigent enough to only exaggerate the discord between the woman and the world she judges detestable enough to want to recreate."[6] Recalling how Breton confides in *Nadja* (where we learn that she began to draw only after meeting him) that he would read Nadja's letters "with the eye with which I read all sorts of poetic texts" (p. 137) makes one point especially noteworthy: after treatment. Aimée wrote no more. Could it be that Breton—who knew nothing about Aimée at the time he wrote his first surrealist manifesto—foresaw what would happen to her and to persons like her, when he spoke in the *Manifeste* of the "futile task" of treating the mentally ill?

Among the first in France, outside medical circles, to be alerted to the work of Sigmund Freud, whom he visited in Vienna in 1921, André Breton attempted (without success, as it happened) to interest some of the elder statesmen of French literature in Freudian methodology. Meanwhile, in a letter dated December 26, 1932 (reproduced for the first time in *Le Surréalisme au service de la Révolution* and then in *Les Vases communicants*), Freud admitted to being quite unclear about surrealism's aims. One must assume that he was just being tactful, since nothing could reduce the distance separating him from the surrealists, so long as they adamantly refused to acknowledge the therapeutic nature of his method and persisted in being attentive to its fruits while pointedly ignoring the purpose motivating its application in the treatment of the mentally sick.[7] The fact is that conflicting aspects of Breton's position with respect to Nadja's condition take us to the essence of surrealist activity.

The moment came in their relationship when Nadja told Breton on October 13 of an incident he judged to be vulgarly brutal. She reported having been struck in the mouth by a man with whom she had refused to leave a bar "simply because he was lower class." Breton relates that he was reduced to tears by the thought that he would not see her again, could not do so. In his eyes, her dignity had been tarnished. So it seemed to him at the time that the incident was in fact "an intimation of the irreparable disaster carrying away a part of herself, the most humanly defined part," by the way (p. 116). Before long, we hear him argue that, in a private nursing home, Nadja might have been "brought back by slow degrees to an acceptable sense of reality" (p. 134). However, he goes on, "But Nadja was poor, which in the times we live in is enough to condemn her, as soon as she takes it into her head not to conform to the imbecilic code of good sense and morality." It is plain that André Breton cannot (or is it *will* not?) divest himself of the fallacious supposition that Nadja actually chose to act the way she did. He has not come to terms with proof of the progress of mental disorders she was quite incapable of checking.

Going back to the first surrealist manifesto, we come upon the declaration, "It is not the fear of madness that will force us to leave imagination's flag furled" (p. 18). This announcement evidences the esteem in which surrealists will hold a faculty that, circumscribed in its action by society's demands upon each of us, around man's twentieth year—according to Breton—abandons him to his "lackluster fate" (p. 16). It is evident throughout the *Manifeste du surréalisme* that Breton identifies madness with the unrestricted exercise of illuminating imagination. When he comes to speak of the insane, therefore, he says quite openly, "That they are, in some degree, victims of their imagination I am ready to grant, in this sense that it impels them not to observe certain rules, outside which the species feels itself under fire, something every man has learned to his cost" (p. 17). At this stage in his discussion of the merits of insanity as liberative of imaginative play, the danger of madness appears to Breton to lie solely in inducing those it affects to conduct themselves in ways that lead them outside social norms, hence in ways that offend society and attract its disapproval.

In 1924 we find André Breton quite content to acknowledge, "And, indeed, hallucinations, illusions, etc., are not a negligible source of enjoyment" (pp. 17–18). He offers no intimation, yet, of the cost to man's well-being of some form of mental derangement. Discussion in the first surrealist manifesto of the conflict between "an imperious practical necessity," imposed by social living, and the claims of the imagination depicts society's demands as negative and represents imagination as entirely positive, even in the extreme form that manifests itself through insanity. On the side of society gather the forces of perdition, while salvation is to be sought, Breton implies, exclusively on the other. Announcing that he intends the *Manifeste du surréalisme* to "return to the sources of poetic imagination, and, what is more, to remain there," he admits readily enough that his exploratory program may go awry. Even so, his confidence is undiminished: "However, a signpost now indicates the direction in that country and attaining the true goal depends henceforth only on the endurance of the traveler" (p. 32).

It is only after free development of imagination has become firmly linked in his thinking with a liberty the mind gains by way of insanity that André Breton starts to examine and weigh the consequences of unreserved devotion to unfettered imaginative freedom. Only then does he take note in imagination of a potentially dangerous undercurrent, capable of tugging man off course, in a direction that it seems quite unwise to follow. At this point, Breton is only too willing to add a word of warning that tempers his excitement over total imaginative freedom, such as we see reflected in his first manifesto: "Imagination alone gives me an account of what *can be* and that is enough to raise the terrible interdict a little; enough too for me to abandon myself to it without fear of being mistaken" (p. 17). By the end of the nineteen-twenties it will be possible no longer for André Breton to write of imagination exactly as he did in 1924: "Where does it begin to become bad and where does the security of the mind cease? To the mind, is not the possibility of error rather the contingency of good?"

In other words, *Nadja* marks an intermediary stage along the road taken by Bretonian thought. Breton speaks offhandedly here of "the well-known absence of borderline between nonmadness and madness" (p. 137). In spite of this, though, admitting that he ought to have been aware of the risk Nadja was running, he has shown on the very page before that, in his own mind at all events, a perfectly clear dividing line does exist. He expresses himself in a revealingly roundabout fashion: "Now I have never supposed she could lose or had already lost the *favor* of that instinct of self-preservation" (p. 136). What instinct? Breton offers a concrete example when reporting that he and his surrealists friends take care merely to turn their heads away from the flag instead, presumably, of having the effrontery to spit on it or—in a spirit of protest— displaying some other form of "eccentricity."⁸

Before we can proceed any further, it is well to probe the significance attaching to the word "eccentricity," used with such apparent casualness by André Breton. We can begin to do so profitably if we pause for a moment over a book that has been virtually ignored, by surrealists no less than by others with far more excuse for not giving it their attention.

PART TWO

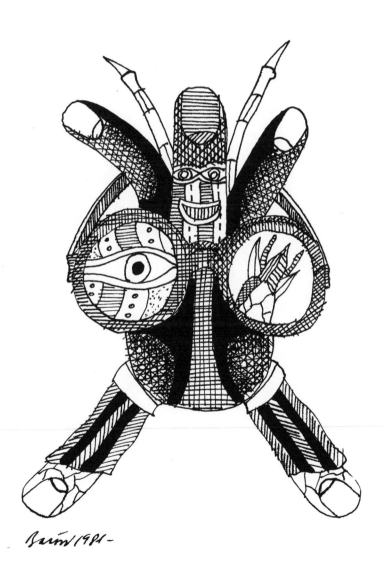

4

"Considerations of Mental Hygiene"

B Y ANDRÉ BRETON'S own testimony in *Entretiens*, after the appearance of his 1924 manifesto, surrealism entered its "reasoning" phase. Intuitions having been collated and hypotheses formulated, it was time for the surrealists in France to begin applying their theories with sufficient rigor to test their validity and promise. And so, in its purposeful experimentation, the period falling roughly between publication of the first surrealist manifesto and composition of the second contrasted with the phase of uncoordinated exploration of possible liberative means that preceded the *Manifeste du surréalisme* of October 1924.

By the time the first number of *La Révolution surréaliste* came out on December 1, 1924, its contributors were agreed on several fundamental points. Among the latter the following in particular are of interest to us: "the so-called Cartesian world surrounding them is an unbearable world, an unfunny practical joke, against which all forms of insurrection are justified. The whole psychology of understanding is brought into question again. There is categorical refusal, on their part, to admit what it has been possible to elaborate from a viewpoint of the mind, in their opinion purely 'cortical.'" To this statement (p. 103) *Entretiens* adds these words: "The only resource was, of course, to oppose the exorbitant pretensions of that 'reason,' which, in our eyes, had usurped the place of true reason and also to preserve impulses and desires from the process of repression, which renders them all the more injurious" (p. 104).

The paramount feature of these remarks is their optimism. They convey a sense of confident purpose that must leave the impression that surrealism followed a steady course, never once rocked by turbulent waters, in the mind of any reader of *Entretiens* who happens to be unfamiliar with the history of surrealism during the period spanned by *La Révolution surréaliste*. It takes a reading of *Nadja* to demonstrate the naiveté of that impression.

Prior to André Breton's chance meeting with Nadja, he and his surrealist friends had concentrated on the positive aspects of mental instability, seeing (or at least presenting) it exclusively as a source of poetic inspiration of enviable richness. Their references to the harmful features of "cortical" reason implied that "true" reason is experienced with least impediment by the insane. Considered this way, insanity appears as a positively productive state with no deleterious effects.

Meeting Nadja reinforced conclusions to which Breton had been led by evidence of grave tensions within his group, originating in their experiments with self-hypnosis. The text of his *Nadja* reveals in its ambiguities that he had not yet resolved all the problems with which mental disorder now confronted him, from the perspective of poetic creative action. It shows, even so, that these problems had already pressed themselves upon his attention and that he could no longer ignore them. This being the case, it is distinctly odd that, many years later, his warm tribute, "Pont-Levis" (prefacing Pierre Mabille's posthumous volume *Le Miroir du merveilleux* [1962]) makes no mention at all of Mabille's *Thérèse de Lisieux*, first published in 1937, almost a decade after *Nadja*.

Mabille's credentials as a doctor of medicine were impeccable—Dr. Gaston Ferdière (who treated Antonin Artaud at the Rodez asylum for three years before his release in 1946) has not hesitated to call him a psychiatrist, even though he too ignores *Thérèse de Lisieux*.[1] Mabille's credentials as a surrealist could never be disputed, either. All in all, then, omission of even a passing reference to the book in Breton's summary of Mabille's valuable contribution to expounding surrealist theory is surprising indeed. Sharpening our understanding of what lies behind *Nadja*, this strangely neglected essay is illuminating on more than one count.

Perhaps the most striking feature of his examination of the case of Thérèse of Lisieux (1873–1897) is that Dr. Mabille does not view it as an instance of exceptional aberrant behavior, falling naturally and exclusively within the province of the trained psychiatrist. Instead, he looks upon motivation emanating from the Christian ethic as providing an aggravating factor in molding Thérèse's conduct, as obviously it does not in Nadja's case, and as operating with enough predictability to make her life history an example he does not shy from terming classic. Mabille, then, dissects Thérèse's psychological condition meticulously, in a way that Breton (who is not qualified to do so) does not attempt to analyze Nadja's. In his own opinion, though, *Thérèse de Lisieux* is more than "a mere psychological analysis," such as any specialist with his background might supply. This is because, being a surrealist, he intends to "lead to an aggressive social critique and proposal of new rules for living."[2] Hence his book stands out as an indictment, unique and all the more impressive for being delivered with authoritative scientific detachment.

Thérèse of Lisieux appears to Pierre Mabille as an individual in whom the pernicious effects of the dualist interpretation of the world proposed by Roman Catholicism (the only form of Christianity with which surrealists in France concern themselves) are to be witnessed "in the domain of love," her destiny being situated, he asserts, "at the exact intersection of christianity and the petty bourgeoisie" (p. 11). To Mabille, all the same, Thérèse—no less than Nadja—appears as "a pathological subject for study." "One passes the boundaries of pathology," he argues, "when this interest in the world diminishes to the point of being reduced to zero" (p. 62). The portrait he paints of her shows Thérèse as a "pitiable victim of the social order and of imposed religious concepts."

The orientation of Mabille's study is significant. Thérèse emerges from his book as a young woman in whom schizophrenia does not progress to the stage of dementia praecox. She exists, all the same, in a schizoid state where psychological isolation and autism are in evidence. Meanwhile objective representation retains only reduced importance for her. The self predominates, living out "a dream without action in which psychological states follow one another" (p. 61).

Psychosis and syphilis are notable features of Thérèse's family history. Meningitis struck her during puberty. Her attachment to one of her sisters (Camille, whom she joined in the convent) is indisputably of a sexual nature, Dr. Mabille assures his readers. As for her devotion to her father, this is seen as Oedipal and as soon transferred to the figure of Jesus. Indeed, Thérèse addresses both her father and Jesus as "Dear King," and writes in her *Histoire d'une âme*, "Now I have no desire left, unless it be to love Jesus madly." Once she has begun to look upon the Christ as both a mystical husband and a child to be mothered, then Mabille judges it entirely fitting to draw readers' attention to "disorders of the sensibility" (p. 48), incontrovertibly betrayed in *Histoire d'une âme*, where we find passages like the following:

Oh! above all, I should like martyrdom! Martyrdom! That is the dream of my youth, because I do not desire only one kind of torture: to satisfy me, I should have to have them all. Like you, my Adored Husband, I should like to be flogged and to die flayed. I should like to be plunged into boiling oil, I desire to be ground up by the teeth of animals, so as to become bread worthy of God.

Thérèse's mental sickness, Mabille suggests, is but a result, and not the key to her destiny: "I have . . . the obligation to underline this coincidence of a morbid state with environmental conditions and especially with christian morality" (pp. 18–19), he declares. Seen from the angle that, as a surrealist, Mabille unreservedly adopts, Thérèse of Lisieux's life takes on the significance of "a symbol of general value and not a curious story or one very personal to an individual" (p. 13).

Mabille's discussion of Thérèse's case history is too intricate to permit of adequate summary here. And after all, it would take us too far out of our way to review the consequences of his announced goal: "examining if any destiny like hers does not deserve to be considered the very example of one of the great natural processes by which humanity is destroyed." It suffices for present purposes to record his contention, formulated apropos of *Histoire d'une âme,* "Not only is the external world vilified . . . but also the whole area of intelligence, knowledge and cognition finds itself reviled" (p. 29). Although dwelling on this fact does not fit in with Mabille's plan, we can see clearly none the less that he detects in Thérèse "an unhinged mind subject to some delirium or other" (p. 24). Hence one interesting aspect of his analysis: without actually being designed to do so, it illuminates Nadja's behavior in a way that André Breton's commentary on what he himself saw that young woman do and heard her say does not. More important still, it elaborates upon the interpretation surrealists in general place on society's response to proof of mental disorder.

Pierre Mabille contends that Roman Catholic dogma encourages masochism in women. At the same time, he asserts, it favors development of schizoid tendencies. These, he goes on to emphasize, are exceptional in Thérèse of Lisieux only because of their intensity. For he sees the "psychological mechanism" to be detected in her as "very widespread thanks to christian permeation of the West" (p. 67). He pushes his argument even farther, to affirm now that bourgeois society develops schizophrenic tendencies. By the time he has done this, his inference can escape no one: "Thérèse is not the first schizoid and will not be the last, but people have not stopped pointing to her evolution as endowed with advantages for humanity or even as a glorious episode" (pp. 69–70).

To comprehend better what is at issue here, one does not have to subscribe blindly to Mabille's conviction that Christianity is "a demonic factory turning out mental debility and the sure road to dementia praecox" (p. 71). All one needs to do, really, is consider the significance of society's awed approval of Thérèse's conduct. As Radovan Ivsic has observed, it demonstrates "what ideological sources nourish banality, that is to say, everything that in the West favors or maintains the misery of the individual, condemned to live, for the past two thousand years, the best of his life in an *elsewhere*, sacred or secular, irreconcilable with the reality of his existence."[3] Things fall into place when we contrast society's respect for Thérèse of Lisieux (beatified in 1923 and canonized in 1925) with its disapproval of Nadja's "eccentricities."

Dr. Mabille depicts Thérèse as exceptional, in fact, only so far as she carries devotion to the self beyond the point where most of us deem it wise to discipline our preoccupations, by refraining from spitting on the flag, for instance, As a result, she appears to personify lack of caution of the sort that André Breton acknowledged as necessary before we can win acceptance in social circles. However, because, in a Christian country, her exceptional behavior falls within the framework laid down by Roman Catholic faith, the influential percentage of the public at large regard it as an example to be treated with respect, if not exactly emulated. The irony of the situation is not lost on the surrealist spectator. He is fully aware of the inconsistencies evident in society's reaction to varying modes of abnormal behavior, and is sensitive above all to the injustice that brings praise and even veneration to Thérèse of Lisieux while sending Nadja of Paris to a madhouse. The one's conduct is found to be admirable; the other's is dismissed as unpardonably reprehensible. In Nadja's condemnation to enforced seclusion (so different in its effect upon her mind from Thérèse's voluntary acceptance of claustration, after yearning for the convent), what counts is that her behavior is judged to be deviant.

The stigma imposed by the adjective "deviant" indicates perfectly well how precarious is the individual's position in a social environment where those around him claim and exercise the right to evaluate whatever he does and to penalize any departure from accepted norms. Stubbornly opposed to the bourgeois society that looks up to Thérèse of Lisieux and draws inspiration from her example of piety, the surrealists cannot but sympathize with poor Nadja. They do so, by the way, in the very spirit of Salvador Dalí, celebrating the conduct of the sexual exhibitionist, whom he describes as committing "one of the most pure and disinterested acts a man is capable of carrying out in our period of debasement and moral degradation."[4] Dalí, it is important to bear in mind at this point, once referred to the typical process of sexual perversion as resembling in every respect "the process of the poetic fact."[5] Less emotionally, René Crevel comments in his "Notes en vue d'une psycho-dialectique," "In the case of sexual exhibitionism or murder, how can we judge without going back to the repression that is at its origin? The beauty of certain acts of indecent exposure . . . is that they bring out in all their violence the monstrousness of laws, of the constraints that make monsters" (p. 50).

Not long before he hanged himself in his studio at the age of twenty-nine (on October 2, 1959), surrealist sculptor and writer Jean-Pierre Duprey approached the Tomb of the Unknown Soldier under the Arc de Triomphe in Paris and urinated on the eternal flame. His gesture of protest and contempt earned him detention by the police (only too willing to display their skill at third degree) and committal to a psychiatric ward. Eleven years later, in Manila on Thanksgiving Day 1970, disguised as a priest, Benjamín Mendoza y Amor (who called himself a surrealist painter), attempting to assassinate Pope Paul VI with a twelve-inch blade, became a surrealist poet overnight. For this "admirable, courageous and unexpected act,"[6] he was condemned to a twenty-year prison sentence. Most surrealists however—even Benjamin Péret, who liked to boast that his hobby was insulting priests[7]—have allowed the instinct of self-preservation that they share with André Breton to impose upon them prudent observation of the social amenities (if not quite respect for them) and due acknowledgment of the norms of social behavior.

The sources of the surrealists' instinct of self-preservation lie very close, it would seem, to those "considerations of elementary mental hygiene" that Breton's *Entretiens* informs us (p. 89) resulted in imposition of controls over the frequency with which, during the twenties, surrealists in Paris held "sleeping sessions," even though the latter had drawn from one of their number the notation, in *Les Pas perdus*, "after ten days the most blasé, the most self-assured of us, remained dumbfounded, trembling with gratitude and fear" (p. 152).

It was Crevel who introduced future members of the surrealist cir- to investigation of the potential of hypnosis for releasing unexpected verbal images. Noted down by a witness, the text called, "La négresse aux bas blancs...," published on November 1, 1922 in *Littérature*, the magazine founded by Aragon, Breton, and Soupault, is a transcription of words uttered by Crevel during one of the sleeping sessions. The only text of its kind ever printed, this transcription supports the argument put forward in Crevel's essay "Après Dada" (*Les Nouvelles littéraires,* February 9, 1924): "To be allayed, the anguish of intelligence needs more than subconscious or spiritist wailing; boldness does not lie in stopping there, but in going always further."

When he came to review *Les Pas perdus* for *Les Feuilles libres* in June of 1924, Crevel (who had recently quarreled with Breton) spoke of feeling that, participating in the sleeping sessions, Breton wished for madness "as for an intake of air." Crevel observed dryly that "madness did not come." And yet in his *Entretiens* Breton was to recall a couple of incidents which he remembered as alarming. He would report that, one evening after dinner, Robert Desnos had to be disarmed when he tried several times to knife his host, Paul Eluard. On another occasion, Breton came upon several acquaintances, all in a state of hypnotic trance, trying to hang themselves—apparently, he notes (p. 90), at the instigation of René Crevel, whose father had committed suicide by hanging.

After admitting that, during the period that has gone down in the history of surrealism as "*l'époque des sommeils,*" he looked upon Desnos as his "mediumistic competitor,"[8] René Crevel once explained:

> Despite the way in which Desnos and I very quickly came to suspect each other, our suspicion changing into an enmity which I thought might lead Desnos to scratch out my eyes, for instance, just as, for that matter, I myself had given him a push which made him knock his head against a mantelpiece—when I meet Desnos on occasions other than those of the seances, these of course are the only thing [*sic*] we can talk about.
>
> When I cannot stand any more, when I realize that I am going to lose my life or at least my head if I go on, I decide as a diversion to have an operation for appendicitis, though not without first having done my best so that Desnos (certainly delighted to have the field to himself) may get more strongly addicted and so go mad. (p. 19)

It is perfectly clear that mental hygiene became a factor to be considered seriously, when the immediate benefits of hypnosis were weighed during the period of exciting experimentation that helped launch the surrealist movement in France. Just as grave—André Breton soon found out for himself—could be the effects of automatic writing upon the practitioner's mental equilibrium. While bringing release from rational controls that he resisted as inimical to free poetic expression, verbal automatism was not without attendant risks. Breton was quick therefore to place restrictions, also, on the frequency with which he himself investigated automatic writing, once he had found it capable of generating, as he duly reported in *Les Pas perdus*, "disturbing hallucinations against which I had to react in haste" (p. 152).

An early participant in the surrealist venture, Francis Gérard, helps explain what had happened to Breton. Writing about "the state of the surrealist," Gérard points out that the exercise of automatic writing submits poets to "a body of sensations and emotions distinguishing this state absolutely from that provoked by any other order of writing." Then he goes on to describe what occurs when experimentation with automatism is interrupted:

> A sort of floating intoxication still disturbs lucidity, at the same time as it is carried away by a virgin fever of activity suddenly taken by surprise and painfully broken off.
>
> Someone who has often lent himself to this exercise can no longer, it seems, detach himself completely from it. Even during the interval between sessions he feels his brain resting on that soft cotton, he perceives that mist floating between him and the precise outer world; once again a subtle poison will open to him the two halves of the doors of a world where, freed, the mind runs in exciting liberty.[9]

Despite the enthusiasm voiced in this passage, the disadvantages of the automatic method are easily discerned. They are implied, too, in a section of *Nadja*. Here we are informed that, one Sunday, the words "BOIS-CHARBON" (which appear on the final page of the automatic texts Breton and Soupault wrote in 1919 under the title *Les Champs magnétiques,* as well as outside business premises in France where firewood and coal can be purchased) granted André Breton the power to "exercise a bizarre talent for prospecting" (p. 25). That is to say, he discovered in himself the unsuspected ability to predict in which streets, and on which side, he would find the sign "BOIS-CHARBON" displayed. He confesses in *Nadja* that manifestation of this inexplicable gift left him feeling frightened.

Commenting pertinently on the "thick railing of spontaneous criticism, often unconscious," that interrupts the flow of words and images rising from the subconscious in Western man, Michel Carrouges remarks appositely:

> It is exact, incidentally, that if one breaks this system of dykes and sluice-gates imprudently, either as a result of a psychic traumatism or by the reckless application of surrealism, consciousness is in serious danger of being submerged by the ocean of dreams, obsessions and madness. It is always hard to explore "terrae incognitae."[10]

Breton's alarm at signs of hallucination in himself is to be set off against his boast—also advanced in *Nadja*—that Robert Desnos' power of speech during sleeping sessions took on "an absolutely oracular value" (p. 29). Only years later would he have occasion to offer some expansion of this brief remark.

During a March 14, 1959, interview used by Jean Barral in his film *La belle saison est proche*, André Breton alluded to Desnos' devotion to surrealist verbal automatism, explaining, "I tried, for my part, to restrain him, the instant I found myself fearing his personal structure might not hold up. Yes, I believe that along this route, beyond a certain limit, there is a threat of disintegration. . . . He bore me a grudge for it, but one had to have been there to know that sometimes he came very close to the abyss."[11] Interviewed, also in 1959, for the magazine *La Tour de feu*, Breton was asked what he had meant, once, by saying Antonin Artaud "had gone over to the other side." In response, he laid down as axiomatic that, "from a certain level onward," poetry "absolutely jeers at the poet's mental health," its highest privilege in his estimation being to "extend its empire well beyond the limits set by human reason." Thus, going over to the other side means "under an irresistible impulse," losing sight of the interdictions that, in society, have "become tacitly a contract" and also of the "sanctions one faces when transgressing them."[12]

According to J.-L. Armand-Laroche, the greatest surrealist of all was Artaud, whom he praises as, "by his morbid state, constitutionally linked to the quest for surreality," a writer "free of all artifice originating in codes, recipes and laws" (p. 102). More exactly, then, among the surrealists only Antonin Artaud succeeded, because he was the only one of the lot whose work Armand-Laroche finds to be authenticated by insanity. The others are dismissed as being "in full mental health," people from whom "that work" demanded "preconditioning." This is to say, if we believe Armand-Laroche, that, "for them, the creation of surrealism was the fruit of logical reflection." In short, Armand-Laroche

attempts by invidious comparison to discredit surrealism, "its philosophy, its ethics, its system of thought." His conclusion: "One cannot
make up one's mind between vanity, naiveté, clumsiness, Machiavelism
or provocation" (p. 97).

These are serious charges, badly misplaced ones. They rest on
Armand-Laroche's fundamental error about the nature of surrealism. He
takes surrealism to be psychosis. If it is not, he implies, then it attempts
to be. Hence any surrealist who is unfortunate enough not to be psychotic inevitably falls short of his goal. One cannot, therefore, advance
with any hope of success toward understanding surrealism's aims and
methods until Armand-Laroche's premise has been dismissed once and
for all as a fabrication, based on crude falsification.

The contrast between Artaud's position and André Breton's is particularly instructive, all the same. There can be no doubt that, in what
he did and wrote, the surrealist leader kept society in view and was
sensitive at all times to the consequences of his actions, on the social
plane. With Antonin Artaud, however, we face something quite different. This is because Artaud condemned society as not merely infringing
upon individual liberty in a way that must be resisted at all cost, but as
quite simply corrupt. Thus he looked upon Vincent Van Gogh as a hero,
an "authentically alienated person." This phrase of Artaud's clearly sepa-
rates alienation from mental imbalance, in that it denies society's right
to pass judgment on man's conduct. The authentically alienated man is
one who "has preferred to become mad, in the socially understood
sense, rather than forfeit a certain higher sense of human honor . . . a
man whom society has not wanted to hear and whom it has wanted to
prevent from emitting unbearable truths."[13]

In Artaud's vocabulary, we may assume, alienation takes on the
value of a deliberate act, directed against society's norms, rather than
involuntary or submissive surrender to an irresistible force that Breton,
in contrast, identifies with the dangerous vocation of poetry. In fact,
Artaud preaches healthy and necessary protest against the accepted aberrations that society condones and promotes, when he challenges the
social values by which certain individuals are found guilty of insane
actions:

> One can speak of the mental good health of Van Gogh, who, his
> whole life long, had only one of his hands cooked and did no more,
> for the rest, than chop his left ear off once,
>   in a world where people eat every day vagina cooked in green
> sauce or flagellated enraged new-born penis. (13: 13)

It is only too clear why Artaud's viewpoint is far from that adopted and defended by Breton. In Artaud's own case, Breton sees contravention of society's code of conduct as a sign that an individual has let poetry push him too far. When Breton treats poetry as having generated Artaud's gift for writing, he does not appear to have paused long enough to wonder whether, in part at least, the latter might not be expressive of mental disorders first declaring themselves while Antonin Artaud was still a teenager. The question is a debatable one, of course. The really significant factor lies elsewhere, though. Breton unhesitatingly weights the evidence in the direction where most support comes for his belief that total surrender to poetic hallucination must be dangerous. There it will appear to reinforce, most conveniently, his contention that conscious control is a necessary regulatory element, protecting the poet's mental equilibrium. By the same token, Breton's display of concern for Desnos' welfare relates unequivocally to his own reservations about spiritism, to which he and the other surrealists first had been introduced by René Crevel: "Contrary to what spiritism has in view—dissociating the medium's psychological personality—surrealism has in view unifying the personality."[14]

Probing the meaning of this last remark, we discover in André Breton's *Point du jour* (1934) a document of considerable importance, shedding much needed light on the motives behind its author's approach to insanity. *Point du jour* shows him persisting in extolling the virtues of insanity—as he and the other surrealists speak of these—while yet determined nevertheless to make sure too high a price is not paid for a share in the benefits enjoyed by the insane artist. In this connection, it is enlightening that Breton's letters to Théodore Fraenkel, written from Saint-Dizier, reveal him to have been far from indifferent to the physical decline only too evident in victims of mental disorders. On August 16, 1916, he referred to "the bitter obstinacy of the foreheads, the dark-ringed eyelids, the eyes carrying that supplication for impossible, unknown help." On the 20th he spoke of prognathous jaws, monstrous potbellies, and stereotyped gestures. A few sentences from *Entretiens* confirm the long-lasting impression made on Breton by his period of residence at Saint-Dizier. It speaks of his "lively curiosity" and "great respect," in the area of mental disturbance. But it confides, too, "Therefore also I learned to forearm myself against this derangement, in consideration of the intolerable living conditions it brings with it" (p. 30).

Given all this, it is especially interesting that *Point du jour* shows Breton to have been quite willing to place the insane in a category where they obviously do not belong at all: next to poets and artists, theologians, psychologists, and psychiatrists. All these, and the mentally ill too, are said to be searching for "a valid line of demarcation permitting isolation of the imaginary object from the real object" (p. 247). It is true that Breton agrees the former "may disappear from the field of consciousness while the latter appears." He grants willingly enough, also, that "subjectively their properties reveal themselves interchangeable." But this still does not reconcile his position with his declaration—made, oddly enough, in *Nadja*—that there exists no real borderline between nonmadness and madness. What is more, if there were indeed such a line of demarcation, we surely could not expect a person subject to mental imbalance to even recognize its existence, let alone seek to plot its course with any degree of accuracy.

Despite an initial air of confusion, things come into clearer focus when we turn, at this stage, to look at what Salvador Dalí has had to say on the topic of insanity in relation to art.

Dalí's exhibitionist nature developed in him, quite early in his career as a painter, a flair for eye-catching titles like that of his essay, "Declaration of the Independence of the Imagination and the Rights of Man to his own Madness." Here we are informed in no uncertain terms that "All men are equal in their madness," since madness is the common basis of the human mind. As soon as we begin looking at Dalí's surrealist writings, however, it becomes essential to grasp that he was not straining after paradox when he announced to all who cared to listen that the only difference between himself and a madman is that he, Dalí, is not mad. Without a doubt, the distinction he drew between his own mental state as a creative artist and that of someone who has succumbed to insanity accounts for the deep impression he made on surrealists in France, when, during the thirties, he devised his paranoiac-critical method.

Nothing could be more misleading than the supposition that surrealists uncritically admire the aimless wanderings of deranged minds hopelessly incapable of facing up to reality. Borrowing from Guillaume Apollinaire the adjective *surréaliste* and deriving from it the substantive *surréalisme,* Philippe Soupault and André Breton immediately gave that word a meaning consistent with their dedication to the task of achieving and communicating a higher sense of reality which came to be known as surreality. This is a sense of the real which, it seems fair to say, no one victimized by mental disorder shares continuously and knowingly, and which nobody ever loses from sight so long as he reaches for the goal to which surrealism aspires.

The signal appeal of Dalí's *La Femme visible* from the moment of its appearance is not difficult to appreciate, therefore. This book, which came out in 1930, expressed its author's admiration for paranoia which, Dalí said, "uses the external world to bring out the obsessive idea with the disturbing peculiarity of rendering the reality of that idea valid for other people." This means that the real of the external world "serves as illustration and proof," and is "placed at the service of the reality of our minds." Dalí's statement of principle, so to speak, is so straightforward that one can only assume Garrabé to have fallen victim to a natural inclination to bend the facts to an indefensible argument. For we hear him contend that Salvador Dalí brings us to "the common object of surrealist and psychiatric research," that is, "elucidation of the functioning of the psychism as support for the Subject-Object relationship" (p. 25). One does not have to listen to Dalí for long to find out that the elucidation to which he is dedicated has very little indeed in common with elucidation as the psychiatrist understands it.

Dalí struck a note that at once claimed the surrealists' attention when he began to stress the inspirational value of paranoia, which he viewed as an intentional denial of the reality principle and so as neither haphazard nor inadvertent. What is most impressive about paranoia, as Dalí spoke of it with imperturbable assurance, is that it appears to be "a delirium of interpretation implying a systematic structure." There seemed to be something really exciting about a "spontaneous method of irrational knowledge based on interpretive-critical association of delirious phenomena." At a time when the surrealists were more than ever before sensitive to their obligation to assume a revolutionary role in society, Dalí's message sounded especially timely and worthy of attention.

A revealing connection links the word "paranoia" in Dalinian parlance with the interpretation Kraepelin placed on the same word. When speaking of paranoia, Kraepelin alluded to a delusion (that of grandeur or persecution, specifically), manifesting itself in a mind otherwise unclouded by any disorder or distortion. Dalí's determination to exploit paranoia in the interest of surrealist investigation and revelation was framed and sustained in that unclouded part of his mind which looked with delight on what occurring in another part, where paranoiac criticism operated. Here, then, lies the source of André Breton's admiration for Salvador Dalí. Like Breton, and just as modern psychiatry does, Dalí acknowledged that paranoid mechanisms exist in all of us. And like the surrealist leader in Paris, too, he sought guarantees of control. Thus Dalí's aspirations in that direction were evidenced in his inclination to stress a delirium of interpretation that implied a systematic structure. Neither to Breton nor to Dalí did paranoid mechanisms appear to be self-perpetuating. Both agreed that those mechanisms must not be permitted uncontrolled activity. Insanity, in other words, appeared to both men as a valuable tool, an instrument to be used in obtaining poetic revelation. We fall deep into confusion, if we do not grasp the significance of the paradox underlying Dalí's emphasis on paranoia, systematized to the point where those availing themselves of it (rather than submitting helplessly to it) can deliberately aim to turn it to good account in surrealism's battle with objective reality.

In the very first number of *Le Surréalisme au service de la Révolution* (July 1930), Dalí's article colorfully titled "L'Ane pourri" (The Rotten Donkey), dedicated to Gala Eluard (whom he first shared with her husband Paul, then married, and eventually painted numerous times as the Virgin Mary), began with the firm assurance: "An activity of moral tendency could be provoked by the violently paranoiac will to systematize confusion" (p. 9). It went on to offer a striking expression of faith: "I believe the moment at hand when, by a process of thought, paranoiac and active in character, it will be possible (simultaneously with automatism and other passive states) to systematize confusion and to contribute to discrediting the world of reality totally." This article of faith rested firmly on Dalí's conviction that a distinctly paranoiac process yields a double image, "that is to say, the representation of an object which, without the slightest figurative or anatomical modification, is at the same time the representation of another absolutely different object, this too devoid of any kind of deformation or abnormality that could reveal some arrangement" (p. 10). In fact, it was Dalí's opinion that manifestation of a third, fourth, or fifth object depends on nothing other than "thought's degree of paranoiac capacity." And that capacity itself, he took special care to emphasize, depends in turn on "the intervention of desire."[15]

In a 1936 essay on Dalí, taken up subsequently in his book *Le Surréalisme et la peinture*, André Breton cited Kraepelin's definition of paranoiac states as corresponding to "the insidious development, under domination from internal causes and according to a continuous evolution, of a lasting delirious system, impossible to shake off, which establishes itself with complete retention of clarity and order in thought, will and action." He quoted at the same time Bleuler's view of delirium as originating in a chronic affective state (based in a complex) that favors coherent development of certain errors to which the subject is passionately devoted. He might have referred his audience equally pertinently to Karl Jaspers' study of general psychopathology, which has been available in French translation since 1934. For Jaspers had pointed out that individuals suffering from paranoia are subject to all sorts of sensory illusions: they hear voices, experience optical pseudohallucinations and coenesthesic sensations. He had stressed that paranoia does not result from acute psychosis, even so. Meanwhile Breton's preface to a Dalí exhibition argued that the artist is a person who has much in common with the paranoiac but yet escapes falling into a psychotic state because he can "*reproduce*" (p. 133). However, the great originality Breton detects in Dalí is that of being "half-judge, half-party to the action brought by pleasure against reality": in fine, Salvador Dalí is both "actor" and "spectator."

What, then, of Breton's claim—prominently displayed in his essay "L'Art des fous"—that the art of those whom society classifies as mentally ill "constitutes a reservoir of mental health"? Are we to suppose, now, that Dalí must be regarded as less healthy, mentally, than he might be, to the extent that he does not share Nadja's condition? Could it be, on the other hand, that the sort of imagination granted the insane is not, after all, the kind on which surrealists may confidently place reliance: "that which tends to become real"?

In his preface to *Surrealism in 1978* Franklin Rosemont speaks of hysteria as offering attractions that "naturally enlisted the sympathies of those who . . . were reclaiming the rights of the imagination and calling for 'poetry made by all'" (pp. 4–5). But how can Rosemont feel entitled to this view, when it is evident that, in the final analysis, the things a madman imagines do not seem to hold out the firm promise of joining all men in the poetic experience; when, on the contrary, it isolates him very often from the rest of us? One cannot answer this question without first recognizing what makes Dalí's work so important to the surrealists. His painting demonstrates its creator's ability to "balance outside and inside himself the lyrical state founded on pure intuition," as André Breton puts it in *Le Surréalisme et la peinture* (p. 135).

Dealing with Salvador Dalí's contribution to surrealist painting, we face "latent" and hence "benign" paranoia. Dalinian paranoia therefore is without the menacing features that made Breton turn from paths appearing to him very likely to endanger the stability of the mind. This, Breton would have us believe, is because paranoiac activity as Dalí speaks of it is regulated by the artist's supervising intelligence. The latter makes its influence felt fruitfully, through the "methodical work of organization, of exploration" by which "raw material" of paranoiac origin is, in a sense, refined. Meanwhile, the hostility that turns the paranoid individual away from daily life is surmounted *"on the universal scale."* Thus, it is permissible to conclude, in Breton's estimation the elements requiring stress in Dalí's definition of paranoiac-critical activity are the first two adjectives finding a place in it: "an organizing and productive force of objective chance."

The signal feature of paranoiac-critical action, as described by Dalí, is that it never ceases to be controllable. "As far as possible," runs a statement in "L'Ane pourri," "from the influence of sensorial phenomena to which hallucination can consider itself more or less linked, paranoiac activity always uses controllable and recognizable materials" (p. 10). This, one may suppose, is why paranoia is able to make use of external reality to "bring out the obsessive idea," while at the same time possessing "the disturbing peculiarity" of rendering the reality of that subjective idea "valid" for other people.

Jean Cazaux evidently was on the right track—that is, the track surrealists choose to follow—when he remarked, in the eleventh number of the magazine *Minotaure* in May 1938, that "a poetic knowledge of the world is above all hallucinatory." Nevertheless, Dalí pointed out, there is still an underlying weakness in Cazaux's reasoning, from the surrealists' standpoint, one that calls for correction. This is why André Breton was so well content to follow Dalí's lead, when arguing in his *Point du jour*, "Secure from all deliriums, one can systematically work at making the distinction between subjective and objective lose its necessity and its value" (p. 250). The key to poetic activity now emerges as systematization, not the haphazard.

How are desired results to be obtained, if not through willingness and ability to follow the example set by Dalí? "In the final analysis," declared Breton authoritatively, "everything depends on our power of voluntary hallucination" (p. 90).

5

Hallucination
INVOLUNTARY AND VOLUNTARY

S INCE Bernheim's study of hysteria and hysterical patients under his care in Nancy, it has been a truism of psychiatric teaching that we are, all of us, as he put it, "potentially or actively hallucinating people, throughout the greatest part of our lives." Acquainted with the surrealist argument that hysteria stands out as a vitally productive means of poetic expression and that—at times, any way—hallucination may be equated with poetic revelation, we face, now, the necessity to confront an important question. Should not our conclusion be, accordingly, that man's capacity for expressing himself poetically must be measured in an upward direction along a scale ranging progressively from potential hallucination up to its active manifestation? Are we compelled at this point to proceed to the deduction that, for surrealists, poetry is the reserved domain of individuals who give themselves over to hallucination—fall prey to it, in fact—without regard for the obligations imposed by society upon anyone who accepts and abides by its norms? It seems as though at least one articulate surrealist asks us to draw that very inference, and to make whatever adjustments then prove necessary in our ideas regarding the nature of poetic expression.

During his period of association with surrealism, Paul Eluard characterized the true poet as *"halluciné par excellence,"* in an essay on Charles Baudelaire where the following informative statement is to be found:

> It must be admitted also that when there is total fusion between the real image and the hallucination it has provoked, no misunderstanding is possible. The resemblance between two objects comes as

much from the subjective element contributing to establish it as from the objective relationship existing between them. The poet, the supremely hallucinated man, will establish resemblances to his liking between the most dissimilar objects (literally he leaves his mark on them), without the resultant surprise permitting, at once, anything but a higher bid. Contagiously.[1]

One does not have to read any farther to appreciate that Eluard is not addressing himself to our questions, and has not quite answered them the way it appeared he might be willing to do.

Eluard looks upon hallucination as a communicative poetic experience no less than a subjective one, familiar then to his audience just as much as to the poet himself. Poetry, Eluard suggests, should not be regarded as anything for the surrealist other than a participative phenomenon, in which the artist's role is well-defined: to draw the public into contributing actively to the creative process. Hence the following definition, proposed in his article on the subject of the physics of poetry: "Poems always have big white margins, big margins of silence in which ardent memory is consumed to create anew a delirium without a past. Their principal quality is not to evoke, but to inspire."[2]

In *Point du jour* André Breton, for his part, challenges a possible error of interpretation when he comments, "'Automatic' or, better, 'mechanical' writing as Flournoy would have had it, or 'unconscious' writing as Mr. René Sudre would have it, has always appeared to me the limit to which the surrealist poet must reach out" (p. 240). Reaching out to a limit does not mean, necessarily, attaining it every time. Nor does it even mean, for that matter, that it should always be reached. And so Breton specifies, "It was a matter, once again, of going as far as possible along a pathway opened up by Lautréamont and Rimbaud . . . and rendered particularly attractive by the application of certain procedures of psychoanalytical investigation." At the same time, his *Point du jour* demands of language a service which gives words the highest possible value: "Once again, all we have is that we are endowed to a certain degree with the word and that, by it, something great and obscure tends imperiously to find expression through us, that each of us has been chosen and designated to himself from among a thousand to formulate that which, in our lifetime, has to be formulated."[3]

With this article of faith, critically important to surrealist endeavor in all fields of creative action, we need to consider a statement made in Breton's *Entretiens* regarding the early surrealists' interest in exploring the subconscious:

Although I was at the time a student of Babinsky's [sic], that is, of the worst detractor of Charcot's theses and of the so-called Nancy school, for my part I still retained a very lively though wary interest in a part of the literature of psychology in line with or hinging upon that teaching; I am thinking in particular of Myers' fine book *Human Personality*, of Théodore Flournoy's fascinating communications about the medium Helen Smith, *Des Indes à la Planète Mars*, etc., even of certain chapters in Charles Richet's *Traité de métapsychique*. All that managed to link and pair up with my other points of view, with the help of my enthusiastic admiration for Freud. (p. 76)

Citing this very passage, Garrabé offers it as proof of "the fact that any surrealist experiment rests on a more solid scientific basis than is imagined" (p. 18). In addition, he contends that it points to the diversity of surrealist theoretical postulations that derive from psychoanalysis. Hence Garrabé reads André Breton's 1933 essay "Le Message automatique" as reviewing the problem of hallucination from Herschel's ideas, in the early nineteenth century, to Pierre Quercy's. Indeed Breton does acknowledge his debt to what William James called the Gothic psychology of F. W. H. Myers, which probes the constitution of the subliminal. And he shows himself duly sensitive to the enigma of "verbal impulsion" and clinical medicine's concern with hallucination, in relation to the philosophical problem of the idea of genius. All the same, Garrabé appears somewhat eager to take the effect for the cause when he deduces that those aspects of surrealist theory paralleling scientific investigation are directly inspired by the branch of science known as psychiatry.

It is important, surely, to note how great a tribute Breton pays psychoanalysis in *Point du jour*, where he says it has succeeded "beyond all expectation" in granting "penetrable meaning" to "those sorts of improvisations" previously considered quite gratuitous, so conferring upon them, "outside all aesthetic considerations," the value of "a human document" (p. 224). But it is even more important to notice that, expressing himself as he does, André Breton avails himself of the vocabulary of psychoanalysis not to confess to its precedence over surrealism, but with the express purpose of bolstering the central argument of surrealism— that true poetic activity has no aesthetic significance.

Neither duplicity nor, to be sure, incomprehension underlies Breton's comments. He is guilty neither of dubious strategy nor of wilful disregard for the prerogatives of the psychiatrist. His remarks are indicative of the distance he has traveled, by the mid-thirties. By now he is well beyond the point where initiation into psychiatric nosography and treatment helped free him from allegiance to poetic forms in which the *rupture* of wartime military service caused him to lose faith.

If, on the other hand, we look a little more closely at Dalí's remarks on critical paranoia, it does not take long to realize how questionable is the legitimacy of his use of the term "paranoia," even when his own delusions of grandeur may seem only too evident. In surrealist perspective, this is no disadvantage at all, however. On the contrary, for this very reason his example stands out as important enough to teach writers something, as well as painters, through his theory of critical paranoia. After all, the goal assigned surrealism, in *Point du jour,* is very clear indeed: "recreating a state that has no reason to envy mental derangement."

For the surrealist, it is not merely a question of setting safe limits on the risks an artist will run, whether he be a painter or a poet with words. Breton surely has in mind achieving—systematically and voluntarily—a state outside the dangerous and confining zone of lunacy, which none the less resembles madness closely enough to ensure certain benefits, prized highly by all surrealists. In addition, he evidently wants the artist to be fully conscious of what he has accomplished, after attaining that state. The artist will be rewarded with full enjoyment of the capacity to evaluate findings made in that analogous state, and by standards he has in common with other people whose mental equilibrium is no more shaken than his own. This is the significance of Breton's remark in *Point du jour* that surrealism's main feature will have been to proclaim "the complete equality of normal human beings before the subliminal message," and to maintain constantly that this message "constitutes a common heritage of which it only rests with each of us to claim his share and which soon must at all cost cease to be considered the prerogative of a few" (p. 241).

Commenting on the manifest "wish to abolish the privilege of licensed poets," behind Breton's statement (where we notice the prominence granted the adjective "normal"), Michel Carrouges observes quite accurately that it marks the surrealists' "deliberate intent to preserve the worlds of the imagination from appropriation to the sole benefit of a few people" and also to "provoke a general invasion of all human life by the marvelous" (p. 168), which is the "heart and nervous system of all poetry," according to Benjamin Péret, surrealism's greatest poet.[4] Actu-

ally, then, Breton's thinking—typical in this regard of surrealist thought
—diverges from Dalí's in one important respect. Citing medical opinion
as his authority, in "L'Ane pourri" Salvador Dalí highlights in the paranoid individual "motives and facts of such subtlety that they escape normal people" (p. 10). The inference is clearly that the artist is—and has to
be—superior to the rest of us to the very extent that his sensibility must
be, according to Dalí's implication, abnormal. Breton, though, remained
true all his life to the poetic ambition the surrealists inherited from
Lautréamont, who spoke of "poetry made by all." Of necessity, therefore, he was committed from the start to a form of poetic expression
accessible to everyone.

Pursuing our inquiry through Breton's comments, and Eluard's
too, we discover soon enough that, while continuing to use the language
of psychiatry, during the thirties surrealists in France had begun to
adapt it unselfconsciously to their own ends, regardless of the distortion
that might ensue. Their expanding ambitions were imposed by a grad-
ually emerging sense of the meaning and value of poetic endeavor. Only
when we bear this in mind can we situate *L'Immaculée Conception* in its
historical place and hope to appreciate what Breton and Eluard really
were attempting to accomplish when they began writing that quite exceptional book.

As discussed in *Point du jour*, the poet's prescribed function transforms him into a man possessed, taken over and controlled profitably by
forces that, however beneficent in some ways, may still imperil the
unity of his psychic personality. André Breton grants as much when
indicating that, "practiced with fervor," automatic writing "leads straight
to visual hallucination" (p. 248). He goes so far as to admit to having
experienced such hallucination personally. Then he invokes, appositely,
the name of Arthur Rimbaud, whose *L'Alchimie du verbe* related, "In
the end I found the disorder of my mind sacred." At Rimbaud's prompting, we recall the twelfth and last issue of *La Révolution surréaliste*.
There "Notes sur la poésie" signed by Breton and Eluard rejected Paul
Valéry's definition of poetry ("A poem must be a feast of the Intellect. It
cannot be anything else"), replacing it with another, far more faithful to
Rimbaud's example: "A poem must be a débâcle of the intellect. It
cannot be anything else" (p. 53). This surrealist definition was followed,
incidentally, by the explanation, "Débâcle: that is, a stampede, but a
solemn one, but a probative one; the image of what we should be, of the
state in which efforts no longer count. . . . After the stampede, every-

thing begins." Breton and Eluard added, "We are always, even in prose, led, consenting, to write what we have not wanted and what does not want, perhaps, even what we wanted" (p. 54). A moment later, they were declaring, "A thing successful is a thing successful only through lack of restraint" (p. 55).

The history of the surrealists' attitude to and application of the automatic principle saluted by Breton and Eluard was to be marked by a distinctly perceptible evolution, partly documented in Breton's references to his own experiments with automatic writing. Before long, determination to avoid the threat of "disturbing hallucinations," mentioned in his *Entretiens,* induced Breton to place his trust in what he called voluntary hallucination. Carrouges's pertinent observation, in his *André Breton,* highlights one central fact: "Far from being a monologue, surrealist automatic writing is in fact, rather, a dialogue between conscious man and the mysteriously lost part of himself which, on the other hand, communicates in secret with the whole universe" (p. 146). Still, it is another surrealist—Jules Monnerot—who most exactly pinpoints the deep significance of Breton's eventual decision to rely on voluntary hallucination: "It could not be a matter of 'undirected thought' but of thought differently directed," commented Monnerot.[5]

Nothing could pinpoint with greater accuracy than the phrase "voluntary hallucination" the radical divergence between the outlook of those advocating surrealist poetic exploration and the outlook of medical practitioners specializing in psychiatry. The unambiguous clarity with which Breton speaks comes between us and easy acceptance of Garrabé's thesis that surrealism is an outgrowth of psychiatry and shares its primary aims and ultimate goals.

Henri Ey's definition of the act of hallucinating, in his *Traité des hallucinations* (1973) may appear unassailable to fellow clinicians: "Objectivation and alienation of the Subject himself from his own thoughts and his own discourse." Yet it scarcely fits in with the characteristically surrealist concept of a form of voluntary hallucination, that is, self-induced hallucination, having a set purpose. Agreement between surrealism and psychiatry on the way to deal with hallucination is just as unlikely. In fact, it is altogether impossible, given the psychiatrist's dedication to therapeutic results and the surrealist's devotion to the principle that, voluntarily practiced, hallucination becomes a valuable investigative device, to be given up only by someone no longer devoted to broadening and deepening his acquaintance with poetry.

It is only to be expected, of course, that to some Breton's key phrase may appear, as it does to the medical profession, to hinge on a contradiction. Yet its self-contradictory nature directs attention to the paradoxical elements in which surrealism's interest in insanity takes root. At the same time, it indicates how surrealists assimilate insanity into the poetic process to which their energies are dedicated. It points to the factor of investigative control about which Salvador Dalí spoke and to which various remarks by André Breton insistently draw notice. For, no less significantly, it shows experimentation with simulation of states of insanity taking its place logically—if not quite predictably—in surrealism's persistent exploration of the poetic potential of verbal language. As Monnerot has implied, the aim is no longer full surrender of control over the wandering mind (as in moments of lunacy), but substitution for the accepted supervisory regulation entrusted to rationality of other methods calculated to bring about results not obtainable by traditional, inherited poetic means.

In "L'Art des fous" Breton bids readers note now common sense shies away from the exceptional in every genre. Common sense makes sure that "the famous corridor" keeping genius "in communication with madness" stays serviceable. This is a corridor, he points out, "along which they lose no opportunity to assure us that artists can walk a considerable distance without being pushed too far" (p. 316). Yet his own deep-seated conviction that the dangers are more serious than most people think urges him to confront a fundamental difficulty, embraced in the following question. To what extent must control be maintained, in the interest of communicability; to what extent must it be relaxed, in the interest of achieving effects that otherwise would escape the poet altogether or, worse still, would send him plunging headlong over the brink of lunacy? The risk is one brought to light quite unintentionally by Henri Ey, when he draws a distinction between the madman as marvelous and the artist as "making the marvelous."

Rejecting Ey's distinction, Gaston Ferdière shows he has missed an essential point. Surrealists are not by any means prepared to go mad, just so that they can become better artists. Far from it, they share the view that resisting the fascination of insanity has to be a prerequisite in the truly creative artist. This is crucial to real understanding of their creative effort, when it is considered in relation to mental disorder. It requires, therefore, substantiation through expansion.

Visitors to the large-scale show called *L'Art brut*, put on at the Musée des Arts décoratifs in Paris, were afforded a rare opportunity to judge for themselves the validity of Breton's bold assertion that Adolph

Wölfli is one of the three or four greatest contemporary masters in painting. Between April 7 and June 5, 1967 the Compagnie de l'Art brut displayed no less than thirty works by Wölfli. These had been chosen from among several hundred executed over a period of thirty years, during which Wölfli also accumulated a pile of manuscripts taller than he was, and produced sheets of musical notations no one yet has been able to decipher. Even at the modest rate of one drawing per year of creativity, the *L'Art Brut* exhibition grants Wölfli's achievement quite generous representation, in comparison with the surrealist shows held, worldwide, since the nineteen-twenties. In contrast, the very first issue of *La Révolution surréaliste* included in December of 1924 a reproduction of a painting by Pablo Picasso, represented also in the very first surrealist group exhibit of November 1925. Moreover, Picasso's work was to be discussed in a section of the first edition of *Le Surréalisme et la peinture*, dating from 1928. In the definitive edition of Breton's book (1965), it receives attention in three more articles, spanning the years 1931–1961. Meanwhile Wölfli is mentioned—and just parenthetically— only in "L'Art des fous," where a small black and white photograph of his decorated wardrobe appears.

The closer and longer we look, the less hope there seems to be of accounting for the discrepancy between the surrealists' expression of admiration for Wölfli and the scant attention they have given his work, whenever the chance has presented itself to show his painting to the public. True, their exhibition *L'Ecart absolu* at the Galerie de l'Œil in Paris (December 1965) did include one drawing by Wölfli, whose productivity as an artist we know to have come to their notice by 1958. Yet on the same occasion Picasso was represented by no less than three paintings.

Although insane art received relatively good coverage in the 1965 show, mad artists still did not number more than five percent of those exhibited: together with Wölfli's single drawing were a soup spoon (from the collection of André Breton) fashioned by an asylum inmate, an assemblage executed by another, a modified magazine cover done by Aloyse (a schizophrenic confined for forty-six years, she did the ironing in the asylum's laundry), and a crayon drawing by Friedrich Schröder-Sonnenstern, whose early years were divided between jail and the madhouse.

There is even more striking evidence of what is involved here. It comes from the catalogue *Surrealism in 1978*. Celebrating the hundredth anniversary of hysteria, the Cedarburg exhibition spread over four rooms, according to a well-established surrealist custom. On this occasion, the catalogue invited visitors to notice, the rooms were arranged "according to Charcot's scheme of the four phases of hysterical attack": preliminary (or epileptoid), the major movements, "passional attitudes" (the title under which *La Révolution surréaliste* printed some of the photographs discovered in the Salpêtrière archives), and complete delirium.

It would seem reasonable to expect delirious activity in art to be illustrated in the last room by paintings, sculpture, and objects gathered in insane institutions. Instead, the items brought together there had been submitted by accredited surrealists (more exactly, by individuals who enjoyed the approval of the Surrealist Group in Chicago and of the Phases Movement). They came from several of the twenty-two countries represented in the exhibit. If certain material difficulties had stood between the organizers and inclusion of art by the insane, none is mentioned in the catalogue. Evidently, the unstated assumption is that complete delirium can be manifested quite adequately in work by people who do not know from first-hand experience what delirium is really like. Supposedly, then, it does not matter at all that the closest a sane artist can come—however loosely we apply the adjective "sane," here—is simulation: a speculative and certainly unauthenticated substitute for true delirium.

One enticing hypothesis of special interest takes shape at this point, brought into focus by Pablo Picasso's enviable reputation among a large public quite indifferent to (when not totally ignorant of) surrealism and the goals to which it is devoted. Should we not entertain very seriously the possibility that, reserving so much space in their exhibitions for works by Picasso, the surrealists may have been attempting to turn his reputation to their own advantage? Are they not guilty, in fact, of seeking approval of their aims by way of a procedure that could be described as reaching for respectability by association? These critical questions direct our attention to the published comments about Picasso made by surrealism's chief spokesman in France.

In the first edition of his *Le Surréalisme et la peinture* André Breton cites Pablo Picasso as the kind of painter surrealists as a group admire most—one who refers to "*a purely inner model*" (p. 4) and conducts us into "*a future continent*" (p. 6). There is nothing especially noteworthy in this, apart from Breton's honest acknowledgment that Picasso's position with respect to surrealism is peripheral, as well as exemplary. One progresses no significant distance, either, in "80 Carats... mais une ombre," dating from November 1961. Here Breton remarks that he and his fellow surrealists are drawn to a "*lyricism*" that sets Picasso at a distance from the Cubist painters (p. 116). Even this, though, hardly teaches us anything new, after the firm declaration made by Breton and Eluard in their "Notes sur la poésie": "Lyricism is the development of a protest" (p. 53). Only when we turn to "Picasso dans son élément" do we discover an essential clue. In this 1933 text, Breton likens the famous Spanish artist to "the migratory bird that in full flight is going to turn its head toward what it is leaving behind," while at the same time going to "try to find its bearings in the labyrinth of its own song" (p. 105). In short, Breton is impressed most by Picasso's "implacable lucidity."

Proof of sensitivity to Picasso's lucidity sends us back to *Nadja,* to read a short passage that captured Dr. Paul Abély's attention, causing him to discuss it heatedly in the *Annales médico-psychologiques: journal de l'aliénation mentale et de la médecine légale des aliénés* (November 1929), where it provoked some debate among members of the French Médico-Psychological Society. The pertinent sentence runs, "I know that if I were mad, and had been confined for several days, I would take advantage of a *remission* allowed me by my delirium to calmly murder one of those, the doctor preferably, who might fall into my hands" (p. 133). Busy accusing André Breton of inciting mental patients to kill those attending to their needs (on the supposition, presumably, that copies of *Nadja* circulated freely in all mental institutions), Abély had no inkling of the true significance of the words he found so offensive.

The message Breton intended to convey is altogether different from the one Abély thought we are meant to hear. Its key lies in the interplay between the freedom of action brought by temporary remission and the adverb "calmly." The latter sounds quite distractingly out of place if one does not perceive the value it assumes in context. Committing a murder such as he imagines, André Breton would be acting with full knowledge of what he was doing and of the interpretation society would inevitably place on his action. With a profound sense of responsibility, he would be carrying out an act society surely would condemn (and punish) as inexcusably irresponsible; that is, as insane. And he would be doing so at the very moment when mental disorder had ceased to cloud his mind, while he was enjoying an instant of full awareness. Under conditions in which he would seek no protection from his well-developed instinct of self-preservation, he would have abandoned caution. It would not matter to him any longer that, to others, his behavior must appear quite irrationally violent. Far more important would be the opportunity to offer a calculated gesture of defiance. In other words, he would not be satisfied just with reacting to his situation blindly. He would need to be fully conscious of the significance of what he was doing. Picasso's lucidity therefore would be reflected in his own.

Breton's careful supervision of hypnotic trance, verbal automatism, and its effects denotes a firm conviction that lucidity must be preserved wherever possible. This is why, in his *Second Manifeste du surréalisme*, he formulated the celebrated article of faith, that everything leads us to believe in the existence of "a certain point in the mind from which life and death, real and imaginary . . . cease to be perceived in contradiction," adding that it is useless to seek any other motive in surrealist activity than "the hope of determining that point" (p. 154). Breton, we readily see, did not aspire to actually attaining the point of which he spoke with such enthusiasm. He merely talked of locating it. His motives come to light on the same page of the second surrealist manifesto, where the following question is posed: "What indeed could they expect of the surrealist experience, those who retain some concern for the place they occupy *in the world?*"

The importance of the words underlined by Breton strikes us when we recall that, by his own testimony, he thought it Nadja's lamentable misfortune not to know any more where she was. Even before their very first meeting, she had reached the state that surrealist activity is aimed at finding, but not at inducing the explorer to enter for good and all. When we read in *Légitime Défense* the categorical affirmation, "We have not ceased to take every precaution so as to remain in control of our research," it becomes clear that continued respect for the work of Picasso is by no means a sign of simple opportunism on the surrealists' part.

In René Crevel's 1932 contribution to *This Quarter* we find:

It is indeed as futile to fix the limits of one's states for the period of sleeping-fits as for any other time. "From Sleep to Simulation"— such even were the words which I had intended to entitle these recollections and simultaneously to embrace the series of experiments which went on until Dali's recent considerations of paranoia (*The Visible Woman*) and the essays on simulation of mental disease (*The Immaculate Conception* by Breton and Eluard). (p. 18)

Examination of the accessible evidence suggests that the distinction Crevel shrugs off as futile is in fact fundamental to appreciation of the logic behind the development of surrealist artistic and poetic experimentation. The latter is carried on outside the frame within which insanity keeps certain artists prisoner, confined to a world of their own. Hence it would appear that *L'Immaculée Conception,* for example, was engendered not by an impulse to drop into lunacy but by the need to investigate an enticing analogy between poetry and insanity. This hypothesis finds support when we detect a curious lacuna, noticeable once we have listed the various anthologies edited by active participants in the surrealist venture.

Next to Mabille's *Le Miroir du merveilleux* stand anthologies of surrealist poems by Jean-Louis Bédouin (1964), Georges Hugnet (1934), Aldo Pellegrini (1961), and Benjamin Péret. As well as *La poesia surrealista francese* (1959), Péret compiled both an *Anthologie de l'Amour sublime* (1956) and an *Anthologie des Mythes, légendes et contes populaires d'Amérique* (1960). Robert Benayoun has assembled an *Anthologie du Nonsense* (1959), while Mário Cesariny has gathered a volume of *Textos de Afirmação e de Combate do Movimento Surrealista Mundial* (1977). As for André Breton, his *Anthologie de l'Humour noir*—its definitive edition appeared in 1966—is among his significant publications.

Breton's anthology, which ran through several expanding editions and covers three centuries, testifies to the importance surrealists attach to the phenomenon he termed black humor. Just like Benayoun's anthology of English nonsense, it has the effect, also, of making us notice that no surrealist has ever undertaken preparation of a representative selection of texts by the mentally ill. This fact seems all the more noteworthy when we recall that none of the surrealists has drawn attention in print to Michel de Muzan's *Anthologie du Délire,* which one might have expected to be bedside reading for a few of them, any way.

The argument that collecting suitable material would have presented some difficulty is no more excuse, in this instance, than it is for the absence of insane art from the *100th Anniversary of Hysteria* exhibition. While at Saint-Dizier, André Breton used to transcribe in his letters to Théodore Fraenkel things said by mentally disturbed patients with whom he had contact. Neither correspondent ever published any of this material, though. So far as is known, Breton never sought to supplement his notes by consulting Dr. Leroy's files. Nor did he avail himself, later on, of documentation that would have been readily accessible to Pierre Mabille. Dr. Ferdière reports that in his own files are "veritable psychiatric observations" set down by Benjamin Péret, of all people (p. 299). Péret never made these public, either. Citing in *Le Surréalisme au service de la Révolution* a medical dissertation on paranoiac psychosis written by his personal friend, Lacan, Crevel alluded to Aimée's writings, praising their poetic nature. Yet he neither quoted

from them (as Ferdière does in his presentation "Surréalisme et aliénation mentale") nor explained why the surrealists have consistently refrained from affording their public the chance to sample the kinds of
insane writing that they respect so much.

Not one surrealist has ever revealed the reasons why writings and
statements by the insane have not appeared to him and his friends
suitable material for collection in anthology form, with or without the
kind of important theoretical introduction to be found in Breton's *Anthologie de l'Humour noir* or in Péret's preface to his anthology of myths
(originally offered in New York as a separate publication called *La
Parole est à Péret* [1943]). Breton lent his support graciously enough
when he wrote "Belvédère," to preface Gilles Ehrmann's collection of
photographs, *Les Inspirés et leurs demeures*.[6] He gladly took the opportunity to ask rhetorically, "Nothing is erected then on the concrete
plane, nothing that can claim some place in the sun outside the norms of
what people agree to consider the 'reasonable' and the 'useful'?" It is
quite evident that he welcomed the occasion to speak up for individuals
who have faced "aberrations in comparison with common sense" and
whose "propensity to 'autism'" has developed alongside concern to project their own world on the physical plane, "with a view to giving it all
permitted expansion." Still, in "Belvédère" Breton did no more than
point out a direction that he himself never took.

It does not seem exaggerated to say we have persuasive proof not
of an opportunity lost so much as of an opportunity surrealists have
elected not to accept. So far as they are concerned, it appears to be no
accident by any means that they have been involved in no compilation of
texts and utterances by people classified as lunatic—even of something
unpretentious (no more than an indication that such material is available
to those who may care to examine it thoroughly) like Michel Corvin's
collection of Dada and surrealist quotations, *Petite Folie collective*
(1966). We are left wondering about their reasons for not bothering to
bring together material by which they repeatedly tell us they set great
store and in which they have found both illumination and inspiration.

Pieces of the puzzle do not begin to fall into place until we look
over a statement by Breton in his article "Entrée des médiums," reprinted in *Les Pas perdus*. Remembering how, back in 1919, his attention
was first attracted to more or less complete phrases forming in his mind
just before he dropped off to sleep, Breton remarked, "It was later that
Soupault and I thought to reproduce voluntarily in ourselves the state in
which they were formed" (p. 149). This notation makes it plain that a
number of suggestive possibilities—including the free association that

patients at Saint-Dizier were encouraged to practice—combined to pre-cipitate a *method* to which Breton and Soupault assigned the name automatic writing, borrowed from a psychiatrist, Pierre Janet. More than this, the method in question may be seen to have held, from the very beginning, the appeal of allowing the practitioner to achieve, vol-untarily, images comparable to those manifesting themselves involuntar-ily. Many years later, Soupault was to comment:

> At that period, while André Breton and myself had not yet baptised ourselves surrealists, we wanted to give ourselves up to experimentation. It led us to consider poetry as a liberation, as the possibility (perhaps the sole possibility) of granting the mind a lib-erty we had known only in our dreams and of delivering us from the apparatus of logic.
>
> In the course of our inquiry we had discovered indeed that the mind released from all critical pressures and from academic habits offered images and not logical propositions and that, if we agreed to adopt what the psychiatrist Pierre Janet called automatic writing, we noted down texts in which we discovered a "universe" unexplored up to then.[7]

Soupault's mention of Dr. Janet is misleading in its brevity. For Janet's *L'Automatisme psychologique* presents automatic writing as a purely involuntary response to predetermined stimulation or suggestion, coming to the subject while he is in a state of hypnotic sleep. Breton and Soupault had borrowed the letter of Janet's theories, without subscrib-ing to their spirit. After all, by Janet's definition madness is "psychologi-cal automatism given over to itself."[8] Thus genius and madness are "the two extreme and opposing terms of all psychological development." Breton, on the other hand, demanded an awareness totally absent from automatic writing as Janet understood it.

Admitting that "an indisputable conventionalism" had begun to sully automatic texts before 1930, Breton commented in his second surrealist manifesto that the fault lay in negligence on the part of its authors, generally content, he said, to "let the pen run over the paper without in the least observing what was happening to them at the time" (pp. 189–90). Not long afterward, in a 1933 article called "Le Message automatique," taken up in *Point du jour*, Breton was to insist on "the precise distinction to be made between the automatism favored by sur-realist painters and writers, on the one side, and the automatism of mediums in spiritism, on the other" (p. 173). It was *L'Immaculée Con-*

ception, though, that gave Breton—in conjunction with Paul Eluard— the occasion to point out most clearly something that, elsewhere, he confined himself to stating only incidentally, without giving it the full emphasis it deserved.

6

Insanity's Poetic Simulation

L'IMMACULÉE CONCEPTION by André Breton and Paul Eluard appeared on November 24, 1930, at a time when, according to Louis Aragon, writing in *Le Surréalisme au service de la Révolution* the next year, "More than ever the surrealists refuse to recognize *art* as a goal."[1] Aragon complained on the very same occasion that censorship was keeping René Crevel and himself out of print, commented on the sequence of events that had led the Paris police to confiscate Luis Buñuel's surrealist film *L'Age d'Or* (1930), and pointed out that *L'Immaculée Conception* had been withdrawn from bookstore display.

There is no reason to suppose unusual circumstances precipitated the treatment from which *L'Immaculée Conception* suffered. One may safely conclude that Aragon—who offered no details about the case—looked upon what had happened to Breton and Eluard's book as no more than part of the mounting evidence of a boycott by which, so he contended, surrealist works in general were being victimized, as a new decade opened. Examination of the volume's contents reveals no unforeseen departures from the ideals regularly defended by the French surrealists or from the original concept of poetry they had made their own. In fact, both Breton's constancy to his principles and his habitual prudence made sure that nothing singled *L'Immaculée Conception* out for punitive action over other surrealist publications of about the same time, like a second collaborative work, *Ralentir Travaux* (1930), he had written in conjunction with Eluard and René Char. There is no fair basis for comparison between *L'Immaculée Conception* and Aragon's violent poem *Front rouge* of 1931. Judged inflammatory ("démoralisation de l'armée et de la nation," was the formal charge), the latter attracted the

71

attention of the authorities, who seized all copies, so giving its author the chance to complain—unjustly, as it happened (his *Persécuté Persécuteur* came out, after all, in October of 1931)—of being denied contact with his public. Indeed, perusing *L'Immaculée Conception*, one cannot but notice that this collection of texts develops from attitudes and ideas consistently defended by André Breton, most recently in his second surrealist manifesto, issued in book form on June 20, 1930.

This does not mean that Breton was any more content to repeat himself, when contributing to *L'Immaculée Conception*, than when experimenting between March 26 and March 30 of 1930 with the collective poems soon published as *Ralentir Travaux*. Throughout his life he would continue to urge his associates in surrealism to be vigilant, to fear complacency, and to beware of compromise. The year 1930 found him eager to explore the potential of verbal language in the hope of expanding its accepted limitations. Therefore there could be no doubt of his interest in the goal to which Paul Eluard referred when writing, in one of the three prefaces to *Ralentir Travaux*, "We must efface the personality's reflection so that inspiration may leap forever out of the mirror."[2] Nor can there by any doubt, either, that for Breton as much as for Eluard *L'Immaculée Conception* took on the character of an investigative venture, undertaken in a direction about which we know him to have been especially curious. Fascination with madness led André Breton to take off in one way rather than another. It was an abiding preoccupation with poetic discovery, though, that prompted him to conduct exploration along the path he and Eluard chose to take, when projecting *L'Immaculée Conception*.

The title of *L'Immaculée Conception* has a precise function, in which wounding religious susceptibilities plays but an incidental if entirely welcome part. In this book, church dogma provides a fruitful analogy for an essential article of surrealist faith. All surrealists regard traditional poetic modes as the equivalent of original sin—intruding, that is, between the writer and attainment of poetic grace. Thus an immaculately conceived poem will be untainted by literary original sin. It will be free of the fault that tempts many an artist to look upon art as an end, rather than as a means. And so granting *L'Immaculée Conception* the full consideration it deserves requires appreciation of the end to which it employs the medium of words.

It is easy to be distracted at this point, if one relies on the guidance offered by Dr. J. Garrabé, who contrives to misrepresent the text in two ways at once. First, his reference to the book as a "stylistic exercise" takes measurably from its importance as a document recording surrealist poetic exploration. Hence, reducing it to a formal exercise, Garrabé implies, on the one hand, the presence and influence of aesthetic intentions and considerations of the kind that all surrealists scorn and regard as adverse to poetry and as impeding its manifestation. On the other hand, his second mistake is consistent with his ambition to persuade his audience that surrealism is but an offshoot of psychiatry, dedicated to resolving the very same questions. To conclude, as this commentator does, that *L'Immaculée Conception* is merely an exercise in style, "opening onto a probe of the scientific knowledge of the period," blatantly exaggerates the evidence. Perhaps there are indeed people who agree that, in Breton and Eluard's book, "what we admire still in our day is the power of the liberated mind passing without hindrance from artistic creation to scientific study" (p. 17). But, we can be sure, no surrealists are among them. No participant in the surrealist venture would countenance the idea that art should be or may be placed at the service of science. In short, Garrabé's attitude distorts *L'Immaculée Conception* by foisting upon its authors a purpose that, incidentally, they themselves never once professed to have in mind.

The *prière d'insérer*—the distributed statement announcing the volume's appearance and scope—is a prime document without which the nature of *L'Immaculée Conception* is harder to grasp. It opens with the declaration that, whereas the first and second surrealist manifestoes set forth "the manifest content of the surrealist dream," this book presents its "latent content." From the moment of its inception, the authors' statement reminds us, surrealism resisted the confinement imposed by rationalism and sought to bypass reason's regulations, its close and oppressive supervision of what the poet is free to say and of how he may express himself. Knowing this makes us attentive at once to the second paragraph of the *prière d'insérer*: "The original wish to *simulate* deliriums, systematized ones or not, will not only have the appreciable advantage of bringing to light unforeseen and quite new poetic forms but also the transcendent effect of sanctioning, in a didactic manner that is exemplary, the free categories of thought culminating in mental alienation." We encounter here clear signs of the consistency characterizing Breton's thought with respect to mental disorder in relation to poetic creation, dating all the way back to August 1916, when he reproduced the following declaration by Constanza Pascal in one of his letters to Théodore Fraenkel: "Disturbances in the association of ideas among those suffering from dementia praecox come down to disturbances in the cohesive power of psychic elements. In poetry, there are often associations by assonance, by contrast, etc., and stereotypes, but each word remains in harmony with the main idea." Breton's firm comment to Fraenkel is memorable: "Still, not always."

Also indicative of the trend in thought that eventually brought André Breton to the threshold of *L'Immaculée Conception* is a remark in his 1920 essay on Bertrand's *Gaspard de la nuit,* reproduced in *Les Pas perdus*: "We know today that there is no 'hysterical mental state' . . . . Charcot had not reckoned with his subjects' gift for simulation" (pp. 96–97). Now, in the third paragraph of their 1930 *prière d'insérer,* Eluard and Breton predict that *L'Immaculée Conception* will remain "the source to which it will be necessary to return in order to recognize [to know again] the power of thought to adopt successively all the modalities of insanity: recognizing that power is equivalent to admitting the reality of that same insanity and to affirming its latent existence in the human mind."

L'Immaculée Conception is an investigative work, Breton and Eluard explain, in the sense that it is a book "by which, in disregard of all genealogy, we enter 'the life of cognition' and pursue the adaptation of cognition to desires, thanks to possessions and mediations, roughly opposed to one another from the social point of view but *dialectically* reconcilable." Just as, earlier, we heard the authors of the *prière d'insérer* borrow the vocabulary of Freud, so now it is the language of dialectical materialism that gives form and direction to their ideas, introducing the one-sentence paragraph closing their statement: "L'IM-MACULEE CONCEPTION is the book of 'ideal' possession."

The structure of *L'Immaculée Conception* is imposed by the ideas that have given it birth. The first section is entitled "L'Homme." It leads us through the principal stages of man's existence, from conception, through intrauterine existence, birth, and life, to death. A second section is called "Les Possessions." Dealing directly with states of mental disorder, it is the only part of the book to carry a titled introduction. The third section is reserved for "Les Médiations," with the subheadings "Force of Habit," Surprise," There is Nothing Incomprehensible," "Love of Nature," Love," and "The Idea of Becoming." The closing section, "Le Jugement originel," begins with an injunction familiar enough to readers of Eluard's *Donner à voir*: "Don't read. Look at the white shapes sketching the spaces separating the words in several lines in books and take inspiration from them."[3] The form will be aphoristic here, as it was earlier in *152 Proverbes mis au goût du jour,* written and published by Eluard and Péret in 1925.

The subsection of "L'Homme" called "La Vie intra-utérine" out-
lines the limits within which Breton and Eluard have chosen to operate.
In a text aimed at evoking intrauterine life, they communicate with their
readers by way of language, a mode of expression totally meaningless
within the frame of prearticulate life in the womb. It makes no material
difference that the sequence of images breaks down here and there,
interrupted by disconcerting nonsequiturs, unassimilable by reason, like
this one: "The shadow of Christopher Columbus . . . is not more difficult
than the egg" (p. 11). The act of recording a succession of images for the
benefit of an audience living a postuterine existence is necessarily a form
of accommodation, since utilization of writing is no less foreign to intrauterine life than that of spoken language. The venture would collapse of
its own weight, if we were to view it as attempting to literally take the
willing reader inside the womb and describe life there. L'Immaculée
Conception would be more than meaningless, its existence a self-elimi-
nating contradiction, if it were not to be accepted for what it actually is:
an effort to project poetically, through language, something that can be
experienced only in the absence of language.

André Breton and Paul Eluard are embarked on an undertaking
that calls for rendering some sense of one world in terms appropriate to
and comprehensible only in another. Here the limited but acutely felt
experience of a child provides the elements of comparison: "My mother
is a top for which my father is the whip" (p. 12). There, on the other
hand, comparisons are made possible through far more sophisticated
verbal conceits: "Of all the ways the sunflower has of loving the light,
regret is the most beautiful shadow on the sun-dial" (p. 11). Whatever
the nature of the imagery running across the page in "La Vie intra-
utérine," however, it marshalls elements quite extraneous to the world
it strives to depict.

To describe a woman's face, Breton and Eluard write, "From
within and from without, it is the pearl worth, a thousand times over,
the diver's death." Then, changing the basis of metaphor, they add,
"From without, it is the admirable slingshot, from within it is the bird"
(p. 12). The process of rendition summons up parallels and analogies
that depend for their effectiveness upon the reader's awareness of one
mode of existence (in which Columbus is as familiar as "the Venuses
whose absent hands caress the hair of poets" [p. 11]), so as to suggest
another, no less exotic to the writers themselves, incidentally, than to
their public.

In "La Vie intra-utérine," then, the central factor is an evocative
parallel, illuminating to the extent that it casts light on one mode of life

by bringing to mind a different one altogether. Viewing what results, we find ourselves facing an ultimately insoluble problem: how to gauge the degree of contrivance present against the writers' spontaneity, as reflected in the language they use to recreate a world we all have known, but of which only one of us remembers anything at all. Presumably Salvador Dalí—the artist who furnished an engraving for the original edition of *L'Immaculée Conception*—alone can authenticate the statement, "I cry out, no one hears me, I dream" (p. 12). For Dalí has assured us that his memories go back to before his birth.

As it turns out, in *L'Immaculée Conception* the apparent conflict between contrivance (affectation) and spontaneity (authenticity) is a false one, since the possession mentioned at the very end of the *prière d'insérer* is "ideal" because voluntary, not involuntary. Already the opening section of the book demonstrates that possession, with which we normally associate the irresistible surrender of free volition, is a state the poet can enter and from which he can withdraw, quite at will. Whereas the twenties will be remembered as the period when, through verbal automatism, the French surrealists came closest to the enviable liberty from restraint known to the insane, the thirties mark the decade during which, having drawn back to a position of safety, they indulged in experiments by analogy which the second section of of *L'Immaculée Conception* consistently show to be simulative in nature.

Now, it is all very well for Breton and Eluard to suggest a sense of conception (since no one quite knows what that feels like, to the unborn child), or intrauterine life. Without reliable documents to provide points of comparison, nobody is going to quibble over the poet's right to formulate his own imaginative flights just as he pleases or feels impelled. But when Eluard and Breton move on to represent "Possessions," the situation changes radically. This is because a certain amount of material by individuals genuinely subject to this or that mental disorder is accessible to anyone seriously wanting to make comparisons. The fact that such material does exist sends us to the introduction preceding "Les Possessions" to see what attitude Breton and Eluard adopt in consequence.

On September 3, 1916, Breton reported to Fraenkel having spent the previous Sunday in the company of someone stricken with general paralysis. Turning with this knowledge in mind to examine "Les Possessions," we find that section of *L'Immaculée Conception* divided into five subsections, five *"essais de simulation,"* essays in or attempts at simulation of mental debility, acute mental derangement, delirium of interpretation, dementia praecox, and, as one might expect, general paralysis.

There is no reason to challenge the conclusion put forth in a dissertation defended at the Faculty of Medicine in Paris: but for his knowledge of mental disorder, acquired in part from direct observation, André Breton "would not have attempted to reproduce specific syndromes." Instead he would have "imitated 'madness' the way the uninformed simulator tries to ape it, in the erroneous image he formulates of it."[4]

One detail of special importance is given prominence in the introduction to "Les Possessions." Breton and Eluard insist on "the absolute honesty" of an "enterprise" consisting, they say, in submitting their *essais de simulation* to specialists and nonspecialists alike. This statement leads to the even more revealing remark that "the least possibility of borrowing from clinical texts or of more of less skilful parody" would be enough to cause such *essais* to "lose all *raison d'être*," would deprive them of all efficacy" (p. 23).

Of course, the vast majority of readers have no direct acquaintance with insane texts by which to judge how well Breton and Eluard manage to simulate states of madness. Quite aware of this fact, the authors of *L'Immaculée Conception* still decline to take refuge behind it. Instead, they point out that it is not in the least a matter of prejudging "the perfect verisimilitude" of the "false mental states" they have to offer— "the essential thing being to elicit the thought that with some training they could be rendered perfectly verisimilar" (p. 24). Otherwise an important target would be missed: disposing of "the vainglorious categories that people amuse themselves by imposing on men who have had no account to settle with human reason, the very same reason that daily denies us the right to express ourselves by the means instinctive to us."

This, then, is the best basis for judgment, indeed the only one. There is no necessity to ask whether, in "Les Possessions," André Breton and Paul Eluard convince any reader they actually are insane. In order to fulfill their ambition as poets, all they have to do is persuade their audience that they sound mad, while yet remaining eminently sane. Hence their goal is to elicit admiration, not mere curiosity or pity. In this connection, placement of an introductory statement of purpose ahead of their *essais* is designed to stress the experimental nature of all that follows. It invites us to examine it as material provided by writers who welcome our evaluation of what they have done, but only from the particular angle recommended in surrealism. Nevertheless, this is still not the full extent of the ambition behind "Les Possessions." The critical question posed in the *essais de simulation* is the following. Writing the way they do, have Breton and Eluard really attained new freedom in their use of words?

"Les Possessions" is not to be regarded as a pale substitute, offered apologetically by two normal people who sadly regret not being mentally abnormal. Its existence indicates clearly that, in Breton's opinion, the center of gravity for poetic action has shifted appreciably. Hysteria may continue to be a poetic discovery all to itself. But its value, at present, lies in supplying an accurate yardstick by which poetic accomplishment can be measured in individuals not actually subject to its effects upon either vision or verbalization. Facing the question raised a moment ago, we see better why, in the end, the results of truly involuntary hallucination, of the sort experienced by victims of certain forms of dementia, appeal less to surrealists than products of voluntary hallucination. Simulation presents itself as something other than a substitute for true madness. It becomes a viable poetic means, ultimately more attractive because—theoretically, any way—available to each of us. Apeing the insane (tactfully called parody, in the introduction to "Les Possessions") is not the aim at all. The purpose of surrealist creative activity is not simply to compete with madness; it is attainment of new levels of communicable poetic expression that no longer leave the writer envying persons afflicted with some kinds of mental malfunction.

"Sacrificing from choice to the picturesque," Breton and Eluard stress, has no more to do with the ambitions underlying "Les Possessions" than the expectation of achieving merely "an effect of curiosity." The undertaking to which they commit themselves rests upon a wish to link "the most paradoxical and eccentric manifestations" with the activities of a "mind *poetically* trained" in writers whose mental capacities and processes are perfectly normal. It is meant to demonstrate that such a writer's mind has the power to "subject the principal delirious ideas to itself at will, without any lasting disturbance being risked," without any danger at all of "compromising its *faculty* of equilibrium" (pp. 23–24). In theory, then, the *essai de simulation* offers an ideal medium through which the writer can hope to meet the demands imposed upon him by his obligation to expand the bounds of poetry, while at the same time protecting himself—as Breton's instinct of self-preservation requires—from the debilitating effects of mental decline.

A glance back to his first surrealist manifesto reveals that Breton's adamant opposition to rational sequence led him to formulate there a statement betraying a prejudice against reason more than a capacity to think lucidly. He furnished examples of echolalia and of Ganser symptom. Then came this comment: "In the very short dialogue I improvise above between the doctor and the lunatic, it is indeed the latter who has the better of it. Since he imposes himself by his answers on the attention of the doctor examining him—and since he is not the one asking the questions. Does this mean his thought is the stronger at that moment? Perhaps. He is free not to take account of his age and name" (p. 50).

Gross exaggeration colors this tentative evaluation. It is true, of course, that someone suffering from echolalia will automatically repeat a single word of a question, rather than reply pertinently. And it is equally true that Ganser symptom is characterized by irrelevant responses to questions posed. In this respect, certainly, individuals manifesting the disorders cited are free, liberated from the social obligation to respond coherently under interrogation. But—especially in the case of echolalia—the answers given are not freely chosen, in conscious revolt against the rules of social intercourse. Rather, they externalize a compulsion, over which the speaker has no control of the kind that would allow the listener to suppose deliberate refusal on his part to meet the basic demands of sustained conversational exchange.

By the time he and Eluard begin work on *L'Immaculée Conception* in 1930, André Breton evidently has recognized how limited, in actual fact, is the freedom conferred by the two "mental pathological states in which sensorial disorders claim the patient's whole attention," for which so much admiration is expressed in his 1924 manifesto. Although he does not bother to qualify his earlier remarks at this point in time, he obviously has progressed some distance, and for good reason.

It would be a major error to infer from the evidence he provides that Breton passes, by force of circumstance, from naive enthusiasm to sober caution in his attitude toward imaginative freedom. Observing in his first manifesto that imagination "is perhaps on the point of reclaiming its rights," he proceeds to comment, "If the depths of our minds contain strange forces capable of augmenting those on the surface, or of struggling victoriously against them, we have every interest in tapping these, tapping them first, so as to submit them afterward, if the need arises, to reason's inspection" (p. 23). The degree and even the place of reason's intervention are not specified in the *Manifeste du surréalisme*. Clearly indicated, all the same, is Breton's willingness to grant reason the privilege of intervening in a way and at a point surrealists will deem acceptable. Confining regulation by rationality is far from the goal he designates. Breton's intention is, quite simply, to show himself ready to permit reason to measure, eventually, results achieved outside its jurisdiction and in stubborn defiance of its rules.

The principal inspiring remark on imagination to be found in the first manifesto is the very one that gives meaning to the practice of surrealist automatic writing, during which the poet finds himself an excited and appreciative witness to "the true functioning of thought." Excluded during the creative process itself, the evaluative sense resident in rationality is brought into play only after the event, when it can permit the writer to assess what automatism has allowed him to produce.

A fundamental need to remain always in control, to be able to identify one's voice as still one's own, and to be aware of what it is doing, of where it is leading the reader, emerges from all this. It frames the experiment recorded in "Les Possessions," giving it direction and purpose. This is why the concluding paragraph of the introductory statement begins, "Finally, we declare that we have enjoyed, particularly, this new exercise of our thought. During it, we have become aware, in ourselves, of resources we could not have suspected up to now" (pp. 24–25). An impulse to defy tradition and to shock traditionalists certainly takes its effect upon the assertion that the *essai de simulation* would replace, to some advantage, inherited fixed poetic forms. This does not detract, though, from the genuine enthusiasm prompting Breton and Paul Eluard to affirm that, from the perspective of modern poetry, they consider the *essai de simulation* "a notable criterion" (p. 25).

When we pass from Breton and Eluard's account of intrauterine existence to that of life in this world, one element emerges as common to both subsections of "L'Homme." The nature of the imagery remains remarkably constant. We find in both texts the same use of words, the very same kind of metaphorical language. In "La Vie" we read, for instance, "From the door that is a hand-to-hand fight to the window that is a scuffle, the floor is a parrot, the ceiling a crow that has been frightened" (p. 16). Even when the authors of *L'Immaculée Conception* are speaking of existence, as it falls within everyone's experience, the same denial of rational association declares itself in figurative language. It would be wrong, therefore, to presume that, writing of "La Vie intra-utérine," Breton and Eluard believe it permissible to attempt communication with the reader in a manner markedly different from the one they deem appropriate to presentation of the life everyone is conscious of living. They concern themselves in "La Vie" with "the memory of the next day, the memory of dreadful adventures in a hanged man's fog." The progress to which they are sensitive as man attains maturity turns him, they assert, against reason: "The vague replaces the determined little by little. . . . Pure eyes of clouds rest on him like a bird on its shadow. . . . He struggles with the vari-tinted cloud that in its folds hatches water-hen eggs, from which are born at an advanced hour duty, chance, the haphazard, trash" (p. 17). And the advantages become clear in the very last sentence: "On all his sensations he slips the handcuffs of a smile" (p. 18).

Interest in insanity and promotion of the poetic virtues claimed for the writing it engenders reflect in "Les Possessions" unrelenting opposition to rationality, to the prevalent assumption that communication on the poetic plane presupposes a meeting on common ground—well policed by reason—in which the poet faces his audience under the beneficent supervision of good sense. They are related directly to the surrealists' refusal to countenance the hypothesis that poetic imagery is, essentially, explicable in rational terms. Surrealism, after all, reverses the proposition that requires verbal imagery to yield up a meaning the rational mind can assimilate without undue strain and translate easily enough into its own terms. However it may have seemed in the mid-twenties, the emphasis surrealists placed on the necessary divorce of poetry from reason is indicative of something very different from stubborn determination to withdraw from contact with others into a world where the incomprehensible reigns uncontested. On the contrary, it tests the theory that, freed of reason's control, language is at liberty to explore the realm of creative imagination and, when doing so, to establish contact between men on a new plane. Here reason has no useful part to play in promoting a fruitful exchange between poet and public.

At first sight, so far as it touches on imagination in its relation to reason, surrealist theory appears flawed by inner contradiction. If use of the poet's reasoning faculties is ruled out during moments of true creative action and is eliminated too throughout the process of fruitful communication with others, then what part is left for rationality to play? The answer is that surrealism accords reason the opportunity to acknowledge what imagination has achieved. Reason is allowed, therefore, to testify that, by imaginative means, the writer can obtain results that must exceed the best efforts of verbal association based in rational thinking. In surrealism, poetic analogy stands outside reasonable association. And this is something the surrealists give reason the chance to discover and acknowledge while it grapples with products of the poetic spirit, nurtured by imaginative play, that source of extrarational energy which poets can tap, just as the insane do.

The special significance of "Les Possessions" is that it offers the *essai de simulation* as a deliberate effort to communicate with an audience whom reason has not enticed out of range or reduced to hostility. Its simulative character is anything but a tacit admission of failure by writers who have to concede their inability to go quite mad. In the estimation of the two men who wrote *L'Immaculée Conception,* simulation keeps the lines of communication open between poet and reader, ensuring that the former neither withdraws—so breaking contact—nor outpaces the latter sufficiently to induce him to try to keep up no longer. If, given the mental condition shared by André Breton and Paul Eluard, we must talk of a compromise—*essai de simulation* balancing mental debility, dementia praecox, and so on—we have to acknowledge at the same time that this accommodation appears to the authors of *L'Immaculée Conception* productive enough to excite them over the poetic possibilities of simulative procedures.

Use of the poet's voice bears witness to a choice, or at least to an ambition that inspires enthusiasm. The poet seeks to enter those places to which "the common herd" despair of "having access" (p. 24). It is in a spirit of optimism not frustration that Breton and Eluard permit "certain confusing intentions" to preside over the pages gathered under the title of "Les Possessions." The negative value of simulation (highlighted from society's standpoint by the wariness of army psychiatrists during wartime) fades away, giving place to a positive force, liberating resources that surrealists consider comparable with those of insanity in its poetic restatement of life.

PART THREE

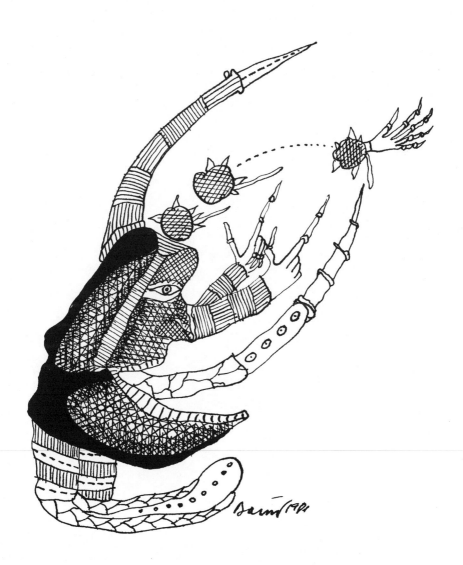

7

Possession

S o much for the theory. Comparison of theory and practice brings less than full satisfaction, while we are reading the opening sub-section of "Les Possessions." An "Essai de simulation de la débilité mentale" displays no real originality of poetic form and substance. But there is some reason for this.

The text as a whole ironically evidences ideological prejudice, an outgrowth of the very premise on which the structure of surrealist thought is erected. Were it not that André Breton and Paul Eluard take themselves so seriously here, one might describe the entire passage as a labored joke, too long in the telling. Their first *essai de simulation* presents mental debility not only as producing craziness (in the form of strange letters addressed to the President of the Republic) but also and concurrently as the source of societal and religious presumptions with which all surrealists violently take issue. So-called right thinking Frenchmen, Breton and Eluard imply, must be out of their heads. How else could those people stoop to give credence to ideas and set store by values enunciated by the imaginary person speaking to us here, some-one whose judgment must have suffered as a result of mental disorder—the only condition under which those ideas and values can appear de-fensible?

The theoretical significance of the text is indisputable. Breton and Eluard make their point with perfect clarity. Only through simulation, their title indicates, could they approach the feeble-minded state in which Western man feels at ease in the world that society has created for him. Only by a deliberate effort appealing to the imagination can they seem to condone living by the principles which they see as inculcated by education in European bourgeois society, supported by religious instruction, and controlled by maxims like "Discipline improves when the leader is just but firm" (p. 27). In fine, "Essai de simulation de la débilité mentale" sets the stage for what follows in "Les Possessions," even though surrealist convictions cannot be said to have inspired, here, use of language that lives up to the grand ambitions announced in Breton and Eluard's introductory note, and even though it does not begin to measure up to the explosive verses of Benjamin Péret's *Je ne mange pas de ce pain-là* (1936), "Vie de l'assassin Foch," for example.

Passage from mental debility to acute mental derangement is achieved, in the second *essai de simulation,* at the expense of sustained rational supervision over thought and its expression via language: "From one bridge to the next, the needles fall like so many saber cuts" (p. 29). More than this, we are conducted into an area for which nothing prepares readers better than acquaintance with Robert Desnos' texts *Rrose Sélavy,* written between 1922 and 1923, and Michel Leiris' *Glossaire, j'y serre mes gloses.*[1]

Throughout "Essai de simulation de la manie aiguë" it is sound, not sense, that opens the road to the poetic virtue of words. Hence, when read only in translation, the following sentence appears to lack acceptable justification, because it develops in a manner that common sense cannot track confidently from phrase to phrase: "The flirting woman's cock-a-doodle-doo brings to life the first lines of the writer's paragraphs." It is permissible to suppose the existence of a somewhat recherché semantic link holding the first French phrase together—"le cocorico des coquettes" (*coquette* being traceable to *coquet,* a 'little cock,' the vanity of the coquette resembling, then, that of the coxcomb). But etymology is of no assistance at all in explaining the rest of Breton and Eluard's statement. Instead, we witness in "Le cocorico des coquettes anime les alinéas des écrivains" (p. 29) the operation of sound association, unhampered by concern for the phrase's development as meaning. Maintenance of sense sequence would be nothing less than a retarding factor in the process allowing Eluard and Breton to make a declarative sentence that moves forward in light of and under propulsion from phonetics, not semantics. Only when sound has been left free to guide the sentence to its conclusion is the thinking mind permitted to intervene, within the limits surrealism prescribes. Only then is it afforded the opportunity to grapple with the poets' statement and to discover that the words consigned to the printed page reward the imagination at the very moment when they puzzle reason and thwart efforts at full rational explanation.

The authors of "Les Possessions" stem the flow of rational thought through language. They divert the sentence from the course to which common sense would commit discourse. And they do so by a simple yet productive method: they listen to words as sounds, instead of hearing them as mere vehicles for sense. Thus the procedure of short-circuiting the current of rational signification is advanced by a mechanical technique, functioning against reason's demands and to the benefit of increased imaginative freedom. Knowingly applied, this technique actively furthers the purpose of simulation by nullifying reason's control over language.

The mechanical nature of the method utilized in "Essai de simulation de la manie aiguë" is not a sign of weakness by any means. Breton and Eluard have no cause to attempt to disguise their operating principles. Imposing an air of greater sophistication would add nothing at all to what they accomplish here. In fact, the opposite would be the case. The second subsection of "Les Possessions" demonstrates how the mind, "*poetically* trained," can avail itself of a simulative procedure fully capable of leading to satisfying results, even though it remains basically very simple indeed. In other words, the prerequisite for poetic creation is not the long and complex training the reader might anticipate after examining the authors' general introduction to their *essais de simulation*. It is, rather, a predisposition to circumvent regulations governing the rational application of language.

The best results, Breton and Eluard give us to understand, come from energetic rejection of the supposition that poetry must yield— eventually, if not immediately—to commonsense explanation. These results follow upon firm opposition to what André Breton once called "the ultradebilitating régime of 'textual explication.'"[2] Productive activity in the field of poetry accompanies concentration upon "that considerable part of creation which ensures the poet assistance entirely different from that of supervised thought, to which aberrant criticism intends, after the event, to submit everything." Meanwhile, "affective communion," he stated categorically, has nothing to do with total comprehension.

Rational thought's natural inclination to follow ideas in progressive order is sabotaged when inconsequential sound associations establish connections to which reason inevitably will remain hostile. Sound reorients the sentence, in the process undermining logical sequence. Thus "Essai de simulation de la manie aiguë" does not display a consistent theme. It does have, though, a discernible structure. The latter is not imposed by the writers' willingness to respect and communicate connected thought. On the contrary, accidents of phonetic association free the mind of reason's enervating tutelage. Haphazard links brought about through sound make it possible for images to develop for their own sake, regardless of rational sequence. By commonsense standards arbitrary enough in appearance to seem nothing of the kind, a fundamental principle is operative here. It is very similar indeed to the principle applied by later surrealists in their collective game called *récits parallèles*.[3]

"The florist kneading flowerbeds is trampling the gardenpaths. For the game that he flushes they are setting up gallows gibbets." In this translation, the words selected to render those in the original have been chosen as the least offensive to reason. Hence, perhaps, they do not always or even frequently communicate the meaning of the text as faithfully as they might. None the less, they do catch some of the surprise generated by the French without, however, revealing the mechanism of surprise, the associative links that make their influence felt by loosening rationality's grip on sentence development: "Le fleuriste qui pétrit les plates-bandes piétine les allées. Pour le gibier qu'il lève on dresse des gibets de potence" (p. 31). This brief extract is typical. As it moves forward, new words suggest themselves, finding impetus in their predecessors. Each successive vocable provides some of the energy that pushes individual phrases onward, in disregard of the requirements imperiously framed by rational thought. In short, language becomes an instrument for exploration, utilized in perfect agreement with the central ambition pursued by the surrealists, who prize the unknown over the known, the unforeseen over the predictable, and the supposedly impossible over the probable.

The more we read of "Les Possessions" the better we appreciate where the interest in insanity really lies, for surrealists. All the clinical aspects of mental disorder slip quietly into the background. Not only is a surrealist incompetent to weigh the significance of these; he is actually not concerned about them at all, since effecting a cure is far from being of major importance to him. Surrealists regard mental disorder as restoring the human mind to productive activity. They see it as creating a situation in which all forms of censorship by rationality are lifted, reasonable objections are silenced, and word pictures are painted with admirable freedom from reason's unwelcome restraint.

The attitude of any authentic surrealist before evidence of creative activity by a person suffering from some form of mental malfunction is one of professional curiosity, so to speak, more than true envy. In 1930 that attitude led André Breton and Paul Eluard to formulate a critically important question. Preparing to write their *L'Immaculée Conception*, they did not ask themselves how it would feel to be insane. Asking, rather, how they themselves might write, if they had fallen prey to this or that mental disability, they went forward from there. Considered from the surrealist standpoint, the "let's pretend" aspect of their experiment in no way diminishes the value of simulation as a viable poetic activity. This is especially so when, as they did, one embarks upon simulation in a spirit of inquiry, with the conscious aim of finding out where insanity leads, without for all that risking losing one's bearings along the way.

The central subsection of "Les Possessions" is an "Essai de simulation de la paralysie générale." Its title sounds far from promising. Indeed, general paralysis evokes depressing thoughts of immobility, of helpless confinement, the static, and even the stultified that seem far removed from the rewarding sense of liberation that surrealists look to poetry to grant author and reader alike. In consequence, the most impressive feature of the text Breton and Eluard bring before us is the fluid movement of images, endowed with quite remarkable mobility of a sort for which the text's unprepossessing title leaves us entirely unprepared.

Presented in the form of a love letter written on the birthday he shares with the "brunette-blonde" he adores, this *essai de simulation* develops through long sentences, meandering across the page, set down by a victim of general paralysis who cares nothing for punctuation. It implies a sharp contrast between physical constraint and imaginative freedom. A sense of domination, attributable to the exciting emotion of love, characterizes the whole passage, in marked contrast with the confinement and dependency to which the hypothetical writer's body must have been reduced. Nowhere better than here do we find vindicated some of the thoughts set forth in Breton's *Les Pas perdus*—the idea that poetry "must lead somewhere," for instance—and the strong conviction voiced in the first surrealist manifesto that poetry "carries with it the perfect compensation for the miseries we endure."

A sense of fulfillment, not of limitation, of joy not deprivation, permeates "Essai de simulation de la paralysie générale": "I roll the diamonds in the moss taller than the forests of which your tallest hair thinks of me" (p. 35). At moments, Breton and Eluard seem entirely willing to depart from the surrealist tradition of respect for grammatical structure. When this happens, they avoid the obvious pitfall: their poetic statement transcends the limits of grammar without becoming incomprehensible. Thoughts of loss, of denial, of sterility, evoked associa-

tively in the healthy mind by the condition of general paralysis are eliminated from what the record shows on the printed page. Such thoughts
are simply irrelevant to the letter-writer's joyous celebration of his love.
Love is inspiring enough to free his imagination, to let him see himself
walking with the woman he adores "in the admirable forests of your eyes
that are accustomed to my splendor" (p. 36). Expressing his wish to
accompany the woman who wants to be his wife along "the beach of
astrakhan" one night, he promises to lead her there "by paths of diamonds paved with primulas of emeralds." He goes on, "and the ermine
cape with which I want to cover you is a bird of prey the diamonds your
feet will tread upon I have had cut in butterfly shape."

Under the beneficent influence of love—which sparked the very
best of Paul Eluard's poetry (postsurrealist as well as surrealist) and led
André Breton to write one of his finest books (*L'Amour fou* [1937])—
images of wonder blossom as though spontaneously in "Essai de simulation de la paralysie générale": "My mouth bleeds on your mouth and
close to your mouth along the pink chestnut trees of the avenue of your
mouth along which we go in the dust to lie down among the meteors of
your beauty that I adore my grand creature so beautiful that I am happy
to deck out my treasures with your presence with your thoughts and
with your name that multiplies the facets of the ecstasy of my treasures
of your name that I adore because . . ." (p. 37). Apparently self-generative, new images usher in others in rich profusion.

In the most salutary manner, "Essai de simulation de la paralysie
générale" combats the prejudice that erects a barrier of suspicion beyond which the sane seek to relegate the insane. We treat the mentally
disturbed or unbalanced (using a vocabulary that is blatantly prejudicial)
as lacking or denied something precious: the privilege of rationality.
Doing so, surrealists bid us notice, we fail to acknowledge the benefits
that come with insanity, with relaxation of reason's hold over the image-
making process.

How successful are Breton and Eluard in simulating general paralysis? For most of us the question remains quite unanswerable. Their
experiment is instructive, all the same. For, their efforts demonstrate
that only by taking thought can a rational human being achieve results
that might bear comparison, on the poetic plane, with the writings of
individuals whose mental qualities we look upon as impaired. The fact
that someone stricken with general paralysis would be physically incapable of writing a letter such as we read in *L'Immaculée Conception* is
beside the point. What is important is the imaginative activity to which
the convention of writing makes us witnesses.

The impression communicated by "Essai de simulation de la paralysie générale" as a written record in epistolary form is that of language moving forward under its own momentum, relieved of the burden of rational logic. Here reasoned thought is incapable of applying the brake, of interrupting or slowing down the process by which words come together in unpredictable images. Moreover, linguistic structures peculiar to French facilitate the evolution of imagery that may sound stilted and even contrived, in translation. We are told for instance that the beach of astrakhan is one that "on est en train de construire à deux horizons pour tes yeux de pétrole à faire la guerre" (p. 36). In English, it is impossible to capture the smooth transitions depending, in French, on the repeated preposition à: "they are constructing with two horizons for your eyes of petroleum enough to wage war." Only upon examination of the pattern of the original sentence may we appreciate the role played by prescribed linguistic form in bringing to light images that can excite the imagination while frustrating reason.

Most often, in the penultimate subsection of "Les Possessions," called "Essai de simulation du délire d'interprétation," another preposition supplies the link between words that rational logic would never bring together. As before, the technique employed is easily identified. And as before it is not the method itself but the result it yields that provides imaginative stimulus. This time the preposition is *de*, a simple connective element used in disregard of reason's expectation. It serves as a steppingstone by which the imagination can advance into the irrational: "Le bariolage de l'averse parle perroquet" (p. 39). On this occasion, *de* precipitates a visual image—a rain shower's gaudy color scheme —that reason will find tolerable, no doubt. Real surprise is released only in the predicate, telling us that the shower's gaudy color scheme "speaks parrot."[4] Elsewhere, though, the images standing out in "Essai de simulation du délire d'interprétation" derive from the linkage of disparate elements, brought into rationally inconceivable proximity by the prepositional *de*.

Reason has a way of judging word imagery with rigorous selectivity, of responding in this or that image to the interpretation it finds most appealing or least offensive. Hence "le carreau du ciel" passes muster when read as "the sky's windowpane," rather than as "the sky's floor tile" (to mention only the commonest alternative meaning for *carreau*). However, reason is powerless to deal with a similarly structured phrase, "l'été de plume," both "summer of pen" and "summer of feather" being resistant to rational assimilation.

The reorientation of thinking which surrealists see as essential to

the poetic experience is central to this subsection of "Les Possessions."
Here we learn that "Le temps *mue*" (p. 40); time, then, is molting.
Anyone who cannot accept this image is welcome to substitute weather
for time and to try out other translations for the verb *muer*: *shedding its
antlers, sloughing off its skin,* or *breaking,* like an adolescent's voice.
Breton and Eluard evidence no patience with nostalgia for the familiar
order of habitual living. The voice to which they let us listen speaks of
"your travels in pigeon class compartments, and the lambs' plinth of
your statues of prey, and your *races of hedges* made at dusk from red-
breasts that are flying away, and the hours, and the minutes, and the
seconds in your heads of green woodpeckers, and your glorious conquests, nevertheless, your glorious coocoo conquests!" (pp. 40–41). This
speaker does not find it enough to repeat that in the beginning was the
word. He maintains, "In the beginning was the song." The song, evidently, is Leda's: "My whirling wings are the doors by which she enters
the swan's neck, on the great deserted square that is the night bird's
heart" (p. 41).

With these words the speaker brings to a close his own song, one
of the shortest *essais de simulation,* leaving informed readers less preoc-
cupied than elsewhere with the question of verisimilitude.

Anyone whose knowledge of surrealist automatic writing extends
far enough will notice, however, that Benjamin Péret made exactly the
same use as Breton and Eluard of the key prepositions *à* and *de,* during
a career as a surrealist closed only by his death. And Péret never represented himself as simulating anything at all. Broad acquaintance with
surrealist writing teaches that, if the authors of *L'Immaculée Conception*
sound mad in their "Essai de simulation du délire d'interprétation," they
sound no more so than Benjamin Péret, Jehan Mayoux, or several other
surrealists who contributed nothing at all to "Les Possessions." Actually,
then, among Breton and Eluard's simulative experiments this one
creates rather than resolves a problem. Reading it as a whole is liable to
leave us in a quandary from which we are less likely—not more so—to
escape when trying to gauge the authors' achievement by scrutinizing
their language against the background of other surrealist writing. For
once, knowledge looks to be an impediment, as we are forced to observe
that no discernible characteristics set this section of *L'Immaculée Conception* at a noteworthy distance from texts by surrealists who have not
felt tempted to try simulating insanity. Thus it appears difficult at first to
situate a passage that we should find less perplexing if it did not sound
quite so familiar.

There is welcome candor in Breton's remarks about *L'Immaculée*

Conception in his *Point du jour* where he pronounces the work successful, with the exception of the "essai de simulation du délire d'interprétation." However, it is plain that Breton is not trying merely to buy
indulgence with a frank admission of failure. Presenting delirium of
interpretation as "delirium of hypertrophy of the reasonable faculties,"
he claims that its very peculiarity prevents its valid reproduction. This
argument may appear to smack of casuistry. Still, the essentials cannot
be ignored. André Breton openly confesses to dissatisfaction with one
part of "Les Possessions." Denied attainment of the elusive goal of acceptable simulation at that point, he and Eluard had to content themselves with writing of the kind to which nonsimulative surrealism already
had accustomed attentive readers.

Instead of hindering us, all this helps set "Les Possessions" in
correct perspective. The provocative claims set forth in the introductory
note to this phase of *L'Immaculée Conception* have to be viewed in
relation to surrealism's general poetic aspirations.

Surrealists take it upon themselves to investigate "the immense
undetermined region over which reason does not extend its protector-
ate."[5] Hence if we treat rationality as plowing the straight furrow from
which the surrealist imagination deviates, then all forms of surrealist
poetic expression can be regarded as manifesting some form of interpre-
tive delirium. Two surrealists, Simon Hantaï and Jean Schuster, once
declared, "Art and Poetry bring to light the irrational by prospecting the
imaginary."[6] Another, Conroy Maddox, pointed out, "By a return to
automatism we see means of eliminating the boundaries and of multiply-
ing the ways of reaching the most profound levels of the mental personality. Painting and poetry become the evocation of a spontaneous and
delirious expression."[7] Similarly, Breton and Schuster commented, quoting Rimbaud without apology or acknowledgment, "I ended up finding
the disorder of my mind sacred."[8] How could a surrealist do otherwise,
when Breton had avowed that, for him, "the only *evidence* in the world"
results from "the spontaneous extra-lucid, insolent relationship established in certain conditions between this and that, which common sense
would hold us back from bringing face to face"?[9]

Surely the best-known set of conditions permitting the surrealists
to conduct their search for poetry are those that make possible the
practice of verbal automatism. Considering the fruits of automatism, we
find a remarkably close resemblance between these and the effects of
hypomania.

Medically defined, hypomania is an illness marked by an accelera-
tion and extension of the subject's stream of thought, bringing about

rapid mental associations. The latter may be, by reason's standards, relevant and logical in character. Just as readily, though, they may be phonic in origin. Hence in hypomania rhyming, alliteration, and punning often establish connections that modify normal thought sequence.[10] In severe cases, unalleviated by therapeutic treatment, complete physical collapse may ensue. Uncontrollably excited, the victim may be driven to incoherence by the free flow of his or her ideas. Not only are hallucinations and delusions apt to occur at this stage, but also violence, intense enough to precipitate homicidal attacks, like Desnos' attack on Eluard, reported by Breton.

All in all, the parallel is too close to be ignored between the state into which the surrealist verbal automatist enters knowingly and purposefully and that into which certain individuals fall in spite of themselves.

Intentionality plays a part in the surrealist *modus operandi* only to the point where it has served to release the poet's mind from reason's control. If we did not know this, we should conclude that typically surrealist poets model their writing on hypomanic discourse, even when the text in question is called *L'Immaculée Conception*. Even though we may dismiss this hypothesis, we are left facing a difficulty which *L'Immaculée Conception* does not come near to resolving.

How may the mind be trained to produce poetic texts that look authentically insane? Concentrating on methodology, we find ourselves in a predicament to which Breton and Eluard indicate no way out. They appear to have thought it unnecessary to provide guidance for readers who are not poets or even for those who may be contemplating following their example.

One of the best commentators on Breton's work, the surrealist Philippe Audoin, highlights the central problem, though not by facing it squarely but in neglecting to address it. Duly stressing that "Les Possessions" is "not at all pastiche but a *recreation* beginning with the poetic training of the mind," Audoin adds, "The same wish to be provocative presided over the choice of the [volume's] title, but the latter rests on a double meaning; the automatic word is in fact the only one whose conception is free from blemish."[11] This summation give no help at all with respect to the nature of the interplay taking place in "Les Possessions" between verbal automatism and the intentionality lying behind poetic training of the mind.

Does not the *wish* to do anything at all by means of automatic writing inevitably contaminate automatism, even violating the automatic principle by overseeing the use of language in a way that can hardly leave it "free from blemish"? The very idea of an *essai de simulation* proves that placement of a heading at the top of each subsection is by no means an afterthought, in this part of *L'Immaculée Conception*. Breton and Eluard set out quite deliberately to simulate certain states of mental imbalance. They did not wait until they had an opportunity to classify various texts after writing them, so as to place under titles they considered appropriate the ones best approximating the mental disorders identified in headings they had selected. Supposing that training can induce the right frame of mind for one *essai de simulation* and afterward successfully adjust the mind to another, then when, where, and how does automatic writing enter into the process? The answer cannot be simply that verbal automatism is purposely excluded from the simulative procedure. André Breton once testified in a private letter that it was not until he wrote his *Ode à Charles Fourier* (published in 1947) that he departed from automatism when writing poetry.[12]

Whatever the explanation, in "Essai de simulation de la démence précoce" language is frequently telescoped. Images do not lead on, one from another, so much as each is absorbed and replaced by the next. Images proliferate over ten lines of text, before the first period allows the reader to pause and take stock, without however having encountered a main verb supporting all the subordinate clauses met along the way. The brevity of the second phrase, only two lines long, permits us to perceive without delay that it, too, lacks a verb. Arrival of the most elementary of verb forms in the third word grouping does little indeed to accommodate reason's demands: "The bucket is notched in heaven by the Virgin immobile in her cask" (p. 42). Rationality will surely judge that incoherence reigns everywhere in this part of *L'Immaculée Conception* and that normal sentence structure has collapsed under the weight of accumulated word images.

The speaker talks of ablating mountains and of "In my thought's thought the big house with working-class houses in the house of human skin with balcony of seals." At this stage, the absence of a verb is scarcely noticeable, so difficult a task is it to visualize a skin house with a balcony of sea mammals. Where grammatical sentences do take shape, it is only to defeat common sense with the message they bear: "God makes me tongues of bread." When verbs present themselves, they assist in reinforcing the impression of disorientation liberated in the reasoning mind: "The ordinary is supreme, although there is some embarrassment in the milk of ovation and evocation." All in all, clarification of grammatical form brings no comfort to rational thought.

Appearing in clusters, images can result from the intervention of the most familiar prepositions at points in the sentence from which reason would ban them: "I caused the germination of myriads of toads' eggs coming from intersections and crossroads of kangaroo stars in the Napoleon-drawered hat of my bureau with feet of leafless clover" (p. 43). Language's capacity to be self-generative is illustrated here. Words can operate freely because the restraints of rational discourse have been thrown off. The imagination follows where language leads, once language is released from the obligation to respect rational thinking.

Grammatical structures are made to function against the rational principles that originally led to their formulation and acceptance. Whether or not the results are entirely typical of the language used by the mentally ill, they are certainly characteristic of surrealist poetic expression by way of words. "Elephants are contagious," runs one of the *152 Proverbes* revised by Eluard and Péret. Meanwhile, simulating dementia praecox, Eluard and Breton affirm that it is cannibalism that is contagious. The aphorism serves as a vehicle for statements that reason can neither accept not yet dismiss as utterly incomprehensible: "You must take the elevator to go from your feet to your head by imagination" (p. 46).

"Quarries [careers? race-courses?] of she-wolves and grey of lead, I've seen everything," write Breton and Eluard (p. 45). "The puffed-up erasers of the perforations on the balloon mail stamps always besiege our good city." Faithful in this to the surrealist tradition, the authors of "Les Possessions" abide here by the established rules of grammar. Hence any reader who cannot accept what they have to say because it rebels against reason is denied the convenient excuse that they do not make sense. Breton and Eluard make grammatical sense, the better to externalize their rejection of rational logic. No one, therefore, can dismiss what he reads in the first three-quarters of their "Essai de simulation de la démence précoce" on the basis that they simply fail to communicate. Use of entirely acceptable linguistic structures merely aggravates reasoning minds, when its purpose is to present nonrational information without ambiguity other than that of fruitful polyvalent sense.

Obviously, these remarks apply to all the earlier parts of "Les Possessions," just as they do to the "Essai de simulation de la démence précoce." So they may be said to define the working method from which this whole section of *L'Immaculée Conception* derives. The last two pages of the dementia praecox subsection break new ground, however.

Abruptly, without explanation, the basis of communication changes radically. Evaluated exclusively by rational criteria, verbal language is not simply misused, here; it misfires. The structure of grammatical discourse is not merely obliged to bear an imaginative superstructure that reasons is powerless to reduce to its own terms. For now neologisms abound, vocables that stubbornly resist translation, the way they defy interpretation except as evocative sounds, only here and there reminiscent of words accepted in the French language as meaningful elements of verbal exchange. Ironically, where traditional sentence form still survives, it is only to give recognizable shape to arrangements of phonemes that exercise their attraction over the imagination through the ear, without submitting to interrogation by reason: "Sous la férule des corrégidors qui marmottent de viges les sumares d'irdienne je passe le soir dans des bocaux sous l'argère des pimons" (p. 47).

To some people this and similar sentences will sound no more than gibberish. Clinicians familiar with the workings of the schizophrenic mind will recognize, however, common ground between the language used at this stage of *L'Immaculée Conception* and that of schizophrenic patients, who frequently coin neologisms in their effort to render their experience. In one sense, therefore, the experiment with language conducted in the "Essai de simulation de la démence précoce" is justified by reference to the model its authors have sought to simulate. From another, equally important perspective, writing such as we have just read tells us to be prepared to witness something more radical than reason's frustration by the nonrational. Eluard and Breton offer us a text that goes on to render rationality altogether inoperative, excludes it in fact as totally irrelevant to enjoyment of the poetic text. It is no longer just a matter of seeing rationality thwarted. So extreme is the reaction against reason's supposed prerogatives, now, that one may say without any exaggeration that a certain degree of training, at least, is demanded of the reader if he is to respond positively and profitably to a statement like "Saute par gloutot." These three words and their arrangement in a sentence of sorts (with a verb but no subject) are so far removed from what reason can project and accept that, by comparison, the next sentence (the third in the paragraph) offers some relief to rational thinking.

This is not because the statement Eluard and Breton have formulated actually meets commonsense standards, but because the reasoning mind is afforded the small satisfaction of observing how rules of grammar function, at this stage, in creating nonrational relationships between words that have found their way into the dictionary with the blessing of the French Academy, and of noting how these words (*rose, retour, retard, ratures, roture*) are interrelated by sound, if not by sense. What results is a sentence that reads, "I ascertained that death [the narrow channel?] was bent on betraying in a burst of laughter and submitting, to the living, night, that pink and white silk of the return of the delay of the erasures [scrapings?] of the commoner's condition" (pp. 47–48).

In "Les Possessions" mental debility is unequivocally placed on the same footing as an admirable form of poetic ability. Hence this crucial section of *L'Immaculée Conception* sets an example to any writer looking for approval from the surrealist camp. It shows him that he would be well advised to divest himself of the restraints and controls upon linguistic expression that generally accepted standards of communication teach us to regard as entirely beneficial and, in fact, as absolutely essential to meaningful and productive dialogue. Proposed and energetically defended by André Breton and Paul Eluard in the name of poetic investigation, a systematic inversion of values finds a new and exciting order in disorder. Among its effects is promotion of mental impairment to the rank of an enviable gift. Meanwhile sanity is repudiated as a barren state, inimical to true poetry. The goal has ceased to be, therefore, lucid formulation of thoughts, ideas, and feelings that a well-intentioned writer consciously aspires to share with others. It becomes instead full and uncompromised attainment of something stimulating to man's imagination, making its impact outside rationality's jurisdiction. This, surrealists contend, language really can encompass only when it functions in unrelenting defiance of the controls exercised over verbal expression by the mind when it reasons lucidly. Or, as the fourth group of words puts it, in the last paragraph of the "Essai de simulation de la démence précoce," "Riason ne hast gler" (p. 48).

8

Game Playing

WHEN A PERSON subject to a state of mental disorder speaks, writes or paints, he or she does so from a spontaneous need for self-expression, intuitively, or at least impulsively. There is no question of knowingly exploring the irrational, out of curiosity or with clear goals in mind: the rational is not being opposed by conscious intent. On the other hand, a surrealist aspiring to write or paint the way irrational people do must resort to studied defiance of reason, actively maintained, or to methods that will oppose reason's influence efficiently. His conduct is motivated by his desire to attain a level of expression which, both in advance and afterward, he associates with achieving a laudable degree of poetic *quality*.

The question of quality, as it applies to the surrealists' pursuit of poetry, merits scrutiny. For Gaston Ferdière's reservations about the surrealists' use of language are misplaced. They turn attention away from what is really important to those participating in surrealism. Essentially, Ferdière's objection is that surrealism inspired "audacious propositions" with regard to language, but "seems to have shrunk from realizations."[1] Citing André Breton's well-known metaphor, "Words are making love," he argues that, in surrealism, they do so badly: "In any case, they do not interpenetrate, they do not break up, they never lose their value as words, as autonomous words, with a place in a dictionary" (pp. 309–10). His criticism that surrealism retains "a certain respect for the dictionary, for the lexicalized word," leads Ferdière to complain that there are few neologisms in surealist writing.

Ferdière selects Antonin Artaud as his whipping boy, lamenting the absence of neologisms in Artaudian writing, though conceding the

presence of "cries, incantations, exorcising rites," and admitting that
delicate analysis of these rites, such as Schelderup has undertaken in
texts by psychopaths, "would bring us some enlightenment." Still, he
goes on to contend that surrealists in general have not profited from the
lesson to be learned from Freud regarding the mechanisms of *condensa-
tion*. Nor, he insists, have they learned from Lewis Carroll's poem
Jaberwocky. One weakness of Ferdière strictures, then, is that they
reveal ignorance of the contrivance underlying the language of *Jaberwocky*, perhaps, more exactly, ignorance of the fact that the deliberation
with which Carroll coined new words is at the opposite pole from surrealist verbal flow. Another weakness is that they attack surrealist language for reasons that betray a mistaken interpretation of the function
reserved for language in surrealism.

Surrealists prospect the irrational with the purpose of attaining the
surreal. It is noteworthy, therefore, that, in Paul Eluard's account of the
"experimental research" initiated in Paris during 1933, not one of the
answers falls short of total, unequivocal coherence.[2] Every one of them
uses language according to the accepted rules at the basis of rational
linguistic communication. None of them either introduces a single neol-
ogism or embodies what Lewis Carroll termed portemanteau words or
even incorporates the sort of word play that is characteristic of Leiris'
Glossaire, j'y serre mes gloses, Desnos' *Rrose Sélavy* or E. L. T. Mesens'
method of titling his collages. Surprise does not follow upon linguistic
manipulation, here. In fact, pedestrian use within the sentence of normal
grammatical structure and of words drawn from everyday usage en-
hances the contrast between content and container. In other words,
disruption is experienced in the mind or feelings without implicating
linguistic framework in the process of frustrating reasonable anticipation.
Meanwhile, in all responses quoted by Eluard, the images evoked point
up the virtues with which surrealists credit irrational vision and its
expression. In short, everything in Eluard's account for *Le Surréalisme
au service de la Révolution* retains the precious quality of communicability, while never submitting readers to the boredom that some of
Nadja's demented remarks generated in André Breton. Without falsify-
ing the evidence Eluard has chosen to bring before the public, we may
say—over-emphasis being permissible here to underline an important
point—that each of the respondents he cites has *performed* adequately
in the answers recorded.

Reviewing Ferdière's critique next to Eluard's account of certain
recherches expérimentales, we make an important discovery. In large
measure, the significance of that series of experiments does not lie quite

where it appears Eluard wants us to look—in the fact that investigation of the irrational was undertaken in the Paris of the thirties "without any preconceived idea of giving it the least publicity."[3] It is important to note, rather, that the surrealists eventually made up their minds to bring their findings before an audience, to share their discoveries with others.

Considering the succession of games in which surrealists have participated over the years helps shed light on the central issue here.

Party games, it is well known, were from the start a characteristic activity among the surrealists. The latter have shown themselves especially curious about the possibilities of poetic action undertaken in common. Specifically, they have always been eager to observe how the individual's capacity for poetic expression may be enlarged by contact with other men and women.

Only years after the surrealist movement was launched did those participating in it discover and acclaim Huizinga's *Homo Ludens*. At that time, the Dutchman's findings appeared to them objective confirmation of their firm belief that man expresses himself most authentically through the poetic act of play. Generally speaking, we can see, the parlor games (to use an unfortunately genteel term that they certainly would regard with suspicion) invented by members of the surrealist circle, or adapted by them to their own needs, present the same fundamental motivation. All were born of investigative intent. They all derived from a curiosity which players expect the rules of the game to assist in satisfying to a remarkably high degree. The confinement imposed and maintained in word games, just as much as in graphic *cadavre exquis*, for instance, is accepted gladly on the optimistic premise that restrictions of certain kinds actually serve to guarantee imaginative freedom. The latter appears all the more productive for being indisputably the result of strictly mechanical means which, in a mood of persistent trust, participants voluntarily apply, with unbounded enthusiasm.

Normally, the games surrealists like to play are of a nature to leave the door open to chance, to facilitate and in fact actively encourage its entry into the field of human experience. Chance is allowed to operate in total disregard of what reason expects and to the benefit, players find to their pleasure, of imaginative stimulation. Significantly mechanical in character, the rules applying in word games, for example, are respected as unquestionably reliable means of eliminating reason's intrusion upon the development of ideas and the flowering of images, of ensuring that imagination is given free rein. By suppressing reason's censorship of verbal expression, the game happily creates a sort of vacuum in which the imagination finds itself released from the gravitational pull of commonsense associations. Thus surrealists look to the practice of certain word games to bring surprises, following with gratifying frequency (if not with complete infallibility) upon strict application of comparatively simple techniques.

Surrealists have never sought to exaggerate the importance of their games. They have never made any attempt to deny that playing affords them fun. At the same time, they have not concealed, either, the faith that game playing inspires in them. On the contrary, they have set much store by the capacity certain ludic experiments possess to advance their investigations. There could be no question of their failing to take their fun seriously, of their ceasing to look to play to effect revelations that only games can bring to light and put within reach.

Given these facts, it is noteworthy that the history of surrealism has demonstrated that those assuming a leading role as spokesmen for their fellows have never even once mentioned to outsiders a single game that yielded results which were, in their own estimation, anything less than provocative and, concurrently, poetically enlightening. A few games, like *cadavre exquis* (in both its pictorial and verbal forms), have proved to be especially popular among surrealists. One form of ludic activity in which they engaged with real excitement, *l'un dans l'autre*, struck Breton as important enough to merit a little book all to itself. Thus it did not merely satisfy the participants' avowed thirst for "diversion," but also proved to be particularly suited to bringing "enrichment under the heading of cognition."[4] The impression left in an outsider's mind by this and other forms of play is that not one game in which the surrealists have found enjoyment has ever failed to offer at the same time the "enrichment" demanded of it. Instead, it would appear that, rising handsomely to the occasion, each has afforded rewarding results, directly related to the advancement of important surrealist ambitions. It seems as though, at any given time, a gathering of surrealists has only to devise a new game, or else try out variations on an old one, to find it instantly productive of poetic material, as well as an amusing pastime. No surrealist game, apparently, has disappointed "the imperious need" to which Breton alludes in *L'Un dans l'autre*: "to finish with the old antinomies of the type action and dreaming, past and future, reason and madness, high and low, etc." (p. 8)—those very obstructive antinomies forthrightly denounced, we remember, in the *Second Manifeste du surréalisme*.

Available evidence does not give us the right to assert that the surrealist record, with respect to the invention of fruitful games, is less than perfect. All the same, what counts is this. Surrealists have never neglected an opportunity to make public the rules of a new game, together with a sampling of the imagery to which its practice has led surrealist participants. Word games, especially, offer enlightenment regarding the manner in which surrealist play brings forth unforeseen images. For surrealist word games are conducted according to rules that actively invite the unpredictable intervention of chance, "a different causality," as Audoin describes it,[5] "more favorable to the degree that it is decided upon and submitted to without appeal." At the same time, the ground rules challenge unwelcome resistance in the reasoning mind to an image's full development. They neutralize the effect of rational thinking, an essentially negative force, in the surrealists' view. Moreover, each game imposes on those playing unquestioning acceptance of a rigid prescribed order that is grammatically impeccable. Therefore grammar ensures in advance that the eventual image will be captured in a linguistic form that communicates to the listener or reader an irrational or antirational mental picture, by way of language that scrupulously observes the rules by which rational discourse is shaped.

Beyond a doubt, among surrealists Hans Arp is the one who argued most vigorously from the basis of firm belief in chance as operating beneficiently in art. Arp worked in painting, poetry, and sculpture completely assured of the demonstrable viablity of the laws of chance. Other surrealists may have defended the same position less boldly. Even so, their creative effort testifies to a faith they share with Arp. We find strong evidence of their confidence in beneficent chance when examining surrealist group activities of a ludic nature. Here chance is granted a central, indispensable role.

During surrealist play the intervention of chance is solicited through rigorous application of agreed rules, without which the benefits of chance would elude man's grasp. As a result, chance proves itself as a reliable instrument for rocking social language at the point where its foundations sink into rationality. Hence chance becomes an unparalleled means by which players in full possession of their faculties can join fruitfully in producing images that, in strangeness, can compete with those inspired by insanity. In other words, chance is to the surrealist preeminently the agent of revelation. Among the sane it serves as a perfectly valid substitute for the state of grace that certain poets find in

their insanity. It is a measure of the admirable gifts of mental derangement, as surrealists view them, that on the plane of poetic creativity
surrealists can vie with the mentally unbalanced only by a concerted
attack on reason, mounted through group action with the critically important aid of chance.

Drawing a distinction between the "ordinary" player of an "ordinary" game, appreciating a "nice shot," and the surrealist at play, Audoin
points out that for the latter a "nice shot" has something miraculous
about it. "It is awaited with secret fervor: its name is 'find' and signifies
'revelation' to the degree that it contributes to a poetic knowledge of the
world and of life" (pp. 478–79).

Surrealists appeal to chance deliberately, rather than letting it
intrude unbidden. And they do so with unwavering confidence that its
intervention in human affairs is invariably beneficent. When playing
games, they rely on certain rules that both solicit revelation through
chance and help break down reason's resistance to irrational postulation.
This means that, with marked irony, they turn to their own advantage
syntactical rules normally considered applicable only to the use of language as an instrument of rational communication.

In games cast in question-and-answer format, the external structure of linguistic exchange promotes confidence in the validity of a relationship between query and response that reason is either reluctant to
acknowledge or quite incapable of perceiving. On the plane of commonsense understanding, question and answer look far apart, since the response has been formulated, as the rules of the game require, in total
ignorance of the question. Thus it is left to imagination to close a gap that
reason remains unable to bridge, so demonstrating what Breton meant
when he said language has been given man in order that he may make
surrealist use of it. Once again, the curious balance between reason and
unreason, between logic and illogicality, appears at the very root of the
surrealist image-making process.

We are now back with the earliest revelations that came Breton's
way while he served at Saint-Dizier. There, encouraged by Dr. Leroy in
diagnostic practice, he had occasion to report to Paul Valéry, in a letter
written August 7, 1916, "My duties all come down to continual questioning: with whom is France at war? and what do you dream about at
night?" More than ten years before "Le Dialogue en 1928," the surrealist pattern of interrogation and unforeseen response appears to have
been set. Even so, the nature of surrealist question-and-answer exchange differs to a noteworthy degree from that in which Breton had
been involved with the mentally disturbed.

When in 1933 Arthur Harfaux and Maurice Henry discussed recent experimentation among surrealists in irrational knowledge of objects, the modifications they proposed in order to improve "experimental research" offered some curious aspects: "People will simply know any question is bad that implies, for its solution, the smallest degree of attention other than that necessary for contact with the object and for comprehending what is asked."[6] How much attention is needed for comprehension? What degree of comprehension, in fact, needs to be attained for the whole experiment to proceed successfully? Lack of precision in these two important respects betrays vagueness no less significant, here, than André Breton's distortion of clinical facts by oversimplification, in his reference to echolalia and Ganser syndrome in his first surrealist manifesto. Surrealists value most, we see, the opportunity to witness imagination bridging the distance between question and answer when it stretches too wide to be spanned by reason, by rational logic. This is why, however achieved, the answers that surprise most, that rational assumptions find least predictable, are those that please a surrealist best.

Here, then, is where the recommendations made by Henry and Harfaux introduce an element absent from the sort of dialogue in which Breton found himself engaging with patients at Saint-Dizier. The kind of spontaneity with which, through oversimplifaction, surrealists credit an insane person replying to a doctor's questions is seriously compromised, once care is taken to allow the sane respondent to be selectively attentive.

No evidence has been recorded that allows us to observe what can happen when someone follows the proposals made by Henry and Harfaux. It is easy enough to see, though, that "Le Dialogue en 1928" promises results far less subject to contamination by reason. This is because "Le Dialogue en 1928" obviates the necessity for even the faintest glimmer of comprehension in the mind of the respondent framing his answer to a given question. The virtue of the dialogue invented in 1928—just four years after Breton declared in his first manifesto that it is to dialogue that the forms of surrealist language are best adapted— has a strikingly productive source. At the moment he makes his reply, the respondent is spared the obligation to be attentive to the question by the rules of the game, which deny him acquaintance with the question he is answering.

In the circumstances, the surrealist's position differs radically from either the therapist's or his patient's. Phrasing a question, the surrealist does not aim to probe his interlocutor's mind. This is why his inquiries often sound gratuitous or even pointless. They can serve no therapeutic purpose, where the rules of the game preclude communicating them to a person required to respond without having been given any idea of what he is being asked. Under these conditions, there can be no hope of collating evidence of pathological states such as André Breton mentions in his first surrealist manifesto, far less of correcting them. The underlying intent is, rather, to take advantage of ignorance. Now, like the "rarefied gases" released by automatic writing that, in the *Manifeste du surréalisme*'s metaphor, allow an electric spark to pass between two conductors set far apart, ignorance facilitates the welcome manifestation of a new image. Taking the place of distraction or obsessive preoccupation in the mentally ill, ignorance creates a situation that yields results comparable—as a source of imaginative liberation—to those surrealists find stimulating in a mental patient's answers under interrogation:

Marcel Noll: What is an umbrella?
Raymond Queneau: The reproductive organs of gastropods.

Marcel Noll: What is fur?
Louis Aragon: The mocking-bird remembering the flood,
        while playing with the shadow of fish.

Benjamin Péret: What is fraternity?
André Breton: It is perhaps an onion.

In each case we witness radical modification of the relationship that answers bear to questions in dialogue resting squarely on rational exchange of thoughts and ideas. Taken off guard at first, the reasoning mind soon learns to be wary of all questions, however innocuous they sound, when experience has indicated that the logical link which normally connects a question to its answer has been severed. By the time a few more example have presented themselves, it appears that there is no link at all between query and response, none, at all events, that reason can detect and interpret. The impression registered in rational thought is that of an inexplicable and inexcusable breakdown between cause and effect. This deduction is soon reinforced by accumulating evidence that can suggest only one conclusion: that no logical sequence connects query and answer in "Le Dialogue en 1928."

Interestingly, when samples from "Le Dialogue en 1928" were published in *La Révolution surréaliste* no indication was given of the nature of the procedure by which answers had been kept too far apart from questions for reason to detect a connection between them. Even when the very same experiment was repeated as "Le Dialogue en 1934," in the special surrealism number of the Belgian magazine *Documents* (June 1934), no accompanying explanation helped readers understand exactly how the basis of dialogue has been transformed. One thing was perfectly clear, all the same.

The few examples cited above suffice to illustrate a feature of "Le Dialogue en 1928" that warrant attention. Whether concerned with some aspect of the physical world (a bed or a heap of stone, for instance) or with values to which society commonly attaches some importance (existence or liberty, for example), every one of the questions posed is flatly banal. The pattern is so remarkably sustained that one cannot but suppose it reflects deliberate choice rather than coincidence. We are certainly a long way, here, from those questions, asked within the framework of "experimental research," that reason has no hesitation about dismissing as preposterous. In "Le Dialogue en 1928" and "Le Dialogue en 1934" a violent break with the commonplace occurs nevertheless, as the response finds formulation. The answers all cut across the categories set up by habitual thinking to accommodate familiar notions and definitions. With the answer the unfamiliar intrudes, abruptly interrupting the flow of ideas to which reasonable reduction has accustomed us and, at the expense of rational sequence, inciting imagination to put banality to flight.

The special significance of the surrealist investigation undertaken for the first time in 1928 is brought into focus in the title under which its findings were made public. It lies in modifying the basis for exchange between men, and hence in changing the force of the word "dialogue." Poetry, we are offered the opportunity to observe, fills a vacuum, the inviting gap between question and answer produced as soon as they have ceased to be correlated on reason's terms.

Among surrealists the fundamental belief shared by all that poetry must "lead somewhere" gave rise without delay to the conviction that spoken language opens a pathway to discoveries obtainable by no other means. Hence the gravity of surrealist word games, which leave linguistic structures entirely free to conduct poetic exploration beyond the zone where reason oversees verbal expression, confining it to the prosaic. Surrealists find here an illuminating contrast between formal rigor and imaginative liberation. For poetry manifests itself not simply in defiance of the former, but actually because of it.

In "*Si . . . Quand,*" each player writes down a hypothetical clause beginning with *If* or *When*, and then a main clause in the future or conditional tense. The latter, it is important to note, while grammatically unexceptionable must bear no relation to the first phrase which, in a normally complete statement, would form a dependent clause. Once this has been done, participants arbitrarily pair off clauses, one from each category. This way they are sure to end up with a collection of grammatically acceptable structures. Not one of these, however, produces a logical sequence that reason can approve.

Where reason denies the validity of the experiment first made public in a special number of the magazine *Variétés* ("Le Surréalisme en 1929"), imagination finds unpredictable stimulation in the haphazard alignment of unrelated clauses. Moreover, the effect produced owes more to the confrontation engineered by chance than to the more or less conscious protest against rationality evidenced in this or that constituent clause:

B.P.: If mercury were to run enough to be out of breath
A.B.: I guarantee there would be trouble.

J.T.: If there were no guillotine
S.M.: Wasps would take off their corsets.

S.M.: When aeronauts have reached seventh heaven
Y.T.: Statues will order cold suppers.

S.M.: If octopuses wore bracelets
B.P.: Boats would be drawn by flies.

Rules of the game of *cadavre exquis* were never outlined, either in *La Révolution surréaliste* or in *Le Surréalisme au service de la Révolution*, even though verbal and pictorial examples were reproduced in both of these publications. Whatever the surrealists' motives in withholding an explanation of how they had conducted their dialogue in 1928 (and again in 1934), in 1929 they showed no reluctance at all to spell out the rules of "*Si . . . Quand.*" It was not a matter of betraying trade secrets but of making one thing clear to all who cared to prove it for themselves. Far from being the prerogative of the insane, surrealist poetry, by collective effort, could be "made by all not one."

As for the answers recorded in Paul Eluard's account of surrealist "experimental research" into the irrational, they illustrate something else very clearly. To those who participated in the venture, denial of certain norms of expression was an offshoot of their unswerving devotion to other norms, set by surrealism. Jules Monnerot's insistence on "thought differently directed," as opposed to "undirected thought," helps point out what is important here, just as it indicates how a phenomenon that is medically inauthentic (simulation of insanity) comes to be considered in surrealism a perfectly valid means of attaining poetry. Monnerot's distinction contributes to disposing of an apparent paradox that may trouble anyone who examines the language used by surrealists claiming to have surrendered control to the irrational.

If we take as an example Eluard's "irrational" suggestion for improving the statue of Alfred de Musset ("Place in front of it the statue of a vigorous exhibitionist, visibly charmed by the muse"), we cannot fail to be struck by his use of euphemism as a device for heightening humorous effect. His response presents a measurable amount of linguistic sophistication, enough at least to persuade readers that they are dealing with a person who has not let himself be shut off in paranoia. Eluard is one surrealist, any way, who, aware of having an audience, actively seeks to meet them strictly on his own terms, and whose first attentive reader is himself. So, while putting his answer into words, he evidently has taken pains to ensure that it will catch and hold the attention of those hearing it or reading it. The tone of his reply is carefully modulated. It betrays studied effect that is significant because it is typical, and not only of Eluard's responses. All the answers to be found in *Le Surréalisme au service de la Révolution* achieve a level of elegance sufficient for their polish to be a factor in the impact they make. All are meant to direct thought away from reason.

When we observe how concern for linguistic form among surrealist game players goes farther than simply meeting the basic demands of clarity in expression, we are ready to notice something else as well.

Salvador Dalí's stress on the voluntary character of what he liked to call paranoia is proof that he was abusing a medical term. Kraepelin's definition of the latter is a reminder of the essentially passive nature of true paranoiac states. If they deserve mention in relation to surrealist goals and methods, the latter are to be placed on the same footing with automatic writing, for example, in which the surrealist's posture is one of submissive receptivity. Thus, accurately identified, paranoia is at the opposite extreme from the aggressive state that Dalí termed paranoia and introduced as the active counterpart of automatism. But this is exactly why Dalí attracted Breton's notice. So-called paranoiac criticism certainly weakens the link between Dalinian paranoia and clinical paranoia. However, it increases the appeal of Dalí's message to anyone who, like Breton, wishes to remain fully aware of his actions, conscious of the poetic virtue of what he creates in light of surrealist aspirations.

The main attraction to surrealists of Dalí's form of paranoia has nothing to do with the sensationalism that has made him the participant in surrealism best known to outsiders. By emphasizing voluntary distortion of external reality through a response mechanism he dubbed critical paranoia, Dalí revealed beyond a doubt that he was not talking of paranoia at all. But that was of secondary interest to those in the surrealist group first hearing what he had to say. What mattered to them was that he came proposing a procedure deliberate enough and purposeful enough to serve as a valuable contribution to the ongoing "rectification of the universe" that Péret demanded of poetry in the name of surrealism. All in all, the paranoia of which Dalí spoke bears comparison with the mode of action provocatively termed irrational by others who, at about the same time in the history of surrealism, drew up suggestions for embellishing the capital of France. After all, they could not but note, Dalí—who did not balk at using the self-contradictory phrase, "the violently paranoiac will to systematize confusion"—defined critical paranoia as "a spontaneous method of irrational knowledge."

Even so, surrealist thought on the subject of irrationality in relation to poetry is crisscrossed with contradictions that not one of its exponents has felt obligated to resolve. Dalí had no explanation about how to reconcile systematizing confusion and use of a spontaneous method of irrational knowledge, and no one else did either. Breton once declared, "We are now at the source of conceptual representation which, our period is beginning to see, derides *perceptive* representation." He did so when prefacing, it is worth noting, Karel Kupka's book on Aboriginal art titled *Un Art à l'état brut* (1962). Yet the notion of art in a brute state, unrefined, does not sum up the surrealist idea of poetic achievement with any degree of accuracy. If it did, game playing would not be the significant feature of productive surrealist activity it has remained between the twenties and the seventies, when the game of *récits parallèles* was invented. And if it did, then the surrealists would not be so selective, in inviting us to admire the work of certain insane artists as facilitating entry into "the life of cognition" about which Breton and Eluard spoke in their *prière d'insérer* for *L'Immaculée Conception*. To its authors, after all, *L'Immaculée Conception* is "the book of 'ideal' possession" because it fulfills conditions they regard as conducive to poetry, bringing glimpses of the irrational universe through simulation, without at the same time imposing surrender to the irrational, hence without requiring either writer or reader to "go over to the other side," as Antonin Artaud did.

All the same, Breton's judgment on Artaud as having fallen victim to poetic hallucination is counterbalanced by his deep and abiding respect for Artaud the poet, despite the differences that caused a rift between them before 1930. On the one hand, as a surrealist André Breton expresses his regard for poetry. On the other, he voices the fear that, without requisite control, poetry may defeat the purpose reserved for it in surrealism, by disrupting the personality instead of unifying it. However debatable may seem the existence of a line of demarcation between madness and nonmadness, one has to grant that, for Breton and his fellow surrealists, such a line exists. They never fail to see it as guaranteeing the poet defense against social sanctions and—even more important—also against the ultimate risks of his vocation.

9

Experimental Research

URING THE MONTH of May, 1933, appeared the fifth number of *Le Surréalisme au service de la Révolution* and also the sixth and final issue of that same French-language surrealist magazine. Among the features of N° 6 was a detailed report on five investigative procedures devised by surrealists resident in Paris. Tried out in February and March of 1933, they all centered on the same ambition, signalled in each instance by the same recurring adjective. The latter gave unity of purpose to the experiments, so justifying their appearance together, in print, as *enquêtes* (inquiries) grouped under the heading of "Recherches expérimentales."

The originality of the games played in 1933 in a spirit of inquiry is that all of them were intended to probe "irrational possibilities" or to foster "irrational knowledge" of the familiar concrete world. In this connection, the trouble taken to give a formal account of them and to publish comments in *Le Surréalisme au service de la Révolution* on the results they had yielded is noteworthy, especially coming so soon after André Breton and Paul Eluard had published their *L'Immaculée Conception*. When one considers the decisive influence of Breton over the investigations conducted in France in the name of surrealism, noting also that the formal commentary accompanying "Recherches expérimentales" was the handiwork of Eluard, it is not difficult to arrive at confident deductions about the reasons why *Le Surréalisme au service de la Révolution* made public the evidence set forth in "Recherches expérimentales."

Of all the games practiced by surrealists none appears to rest on simpler rules than those about which we learn in *Le Surréalisme au service de la Révolution*. The impression is deceptive, all the same. Their very simplicity marks a notable departure both in method and purpose, placing the games called "Recherches expérimentales" in a category of their own.

Preliminary examination establishes that each of them has the same quite elementary format. Participants are required to reply without premeditation—their responses are emphatically termed "automatic" in Eluard's commentary—when presented with a succession of questions, varying in number from one game to another. Still, they respond within a framework set up, in advance, so as to give a definite orientation to the inquiry in which all the players find themselves engaged.

We can arrive at this conclusion about "Recherches expérimentales" only inductively. As a commentator, Paul Eluard turns out to be decidedly vague in his account. He tells us little about how the games were played, concentrating more on analyzing and evaluating responses they had elicited. The most he appears willing to do is assure his readers, under the laconic heading of "Remarques," that the authenticity of all these forms of experimental research is guaranteed by the participants' "maximum seriousness and passionate scrupulousness," and also by the fact that these experiments were undertaken "with no preconceived idea of giving them the least publicity." He does not even state whether answers were delivered orally. We can only infer from his remarks that in fact they were written down: phonic associations such as he mentions occur exclusively within a single individual's responses, never between one person's answers and another's. We have to wait until Arthur Harfaux and Maurice Henry append some observations of their own on the irrational knowledge of objects to learn the following: "an object, preferably simple, not too manufactured, was chosen, and laid on the table. It presented generally a fairly obvious poetic character (coral, a piece of pink velvet). A list of questions was established in common, a list serving later for experiments upon other objects. Then we answered each of the questions in writing; the answers were read out, with a brief comparison, before going on [*sic*] to the next question" (p. 23).

Even this relatively straightforward explanation raises more questions than it resolves. Especially important is its lack of information about the surrealists' basis for selecting questions to be asked apropos of the chosen object. Without some reliable, explicit indications, one cannot know how deliberately participants' attention was directed to the irrational (or was intended to be so directed). A similar vagueness manifests itself with regard to the agreed conditions for participation in one game or another. Were players strictly enjoined to reply only irrationally? If they indeed were, then how did they manage to meet this condition? In any case how, if at all, were they to regulate their uniformly coherent replies? Eluard frankly announces, early on, that his report omits responses presenting "little or no interest." He does not indicate, even so, who was authorized to measure their interest, and on what grounds, specifically. He has nothing at all to say, we notice, about the gaps opening up at various points on the answer sheets. Do these prove, in every instance, that the individual's mind remained blank before this or that question? Or do they reveal, sometimes at least, that he did not judge the reply that suggested itself worth recording? If this happens to have been the case, what were his grounds for rejection?

This last query is of capital importance. It brings us to the fundamental matter of the positive, productive relationship between question and answer in "Recherches expérimentales." More precisely, it leaves us wondering about the nature of the responses that the questions posed were meant to elicit. Eluard's text touches on this only obliquely, and in quite a tantalizing way. It declares categorically that irrational knowledge of an object cannot be acquired except on a subjective basis, and, moreover, "by a single question and a single answer." Eluard refrains, all the same, from explaining why this process should be so remarkably efficient; how, exactly, it leads to desired results. Instead, he makes a somewhat contradictory remark:

> but it is evident that to redetermine this object objectively afterward, it would have been necessary to ask many more questions than have been posed in these *essais* [the French word has been retained to show that it is the very word used by Eluard and Breton when talking of their *essais de simulation*]. In the same way, for the irrational possibilities of penetration and orientation in a picture or for those of life at some date or other, one should almost, on the basis of responses already obtained, and successively, endlessly, pose so many questions that the universe in which that particular place and date participate would be reconstructed. (p. 20)

At least as much, therefore, depends on the questions as on the answers. With respect to certain experiments, at all events, questions have to be selected in such a fashion as to solicit responses that will lead progressively away from the rational in the attractive direction of the irrational, toward something that Eluard openly terms "a certain irrational objectivity with which we could easily be content."

Although the general principle is familiar enough not to appear ambiguous, in the absence of a clear methodological definition we are at a loss to know just which way the surrealists are headed and why it is they have chosen the direction they now are following. Meanwhile, to the outsider their goal continues to be oddly elusive. He has no means of ascertaining what measure of irrational objectivity satisfies their needs, or even for that matter whether the irrational in any form lends itself without vigorous resistance to gradations such as Paul Eluard seems to take for granted. In the circumstances, nonsurrealists can do no more, really, than speculate indecisively about the presumably almost endless continuity Eluard posits between questions and answers and sees as unerringly leading forward in the right direction, not backward in the wrong. Our main aggravation, then, is being without sure information on this essential question: What is the role of rational logic in the method by which questions are selected and ordered with the express purpose of bringing the irrational into sight? The closer one examines the account provided by Eluard, the harder it becomes to answer with assurance the basic questions that "Recherches expérimentales" prompts us to raise.

Initially, the whole matter does not seem to be unduly complicated. Determined to probe the irrational possibilities of life at a remote historical date, those playing selected the digits 409 by lot. It is obvious, then, that the date chosen held no commanding appeal for any of them before he joined in the game. On the other hand, it is not difficult at all to guess why the clairvoyant's crystal ball should have been the very first object used in the game played on February 5, 1933. From the early nineteen-twenties onward, the first surrealists—having no interest at all in the spirit world and with no faith in an afterlife—were fascinated by the idea of penetrating the veil, attracted to the thought of divination. It is scarcely more surprising that, on February 11, they now turned their attention to a piece of velvet. The kinds of responses provoked by that object bear out the erotic suggestiveness the players found in pink velvet. As for exploring certain possibilities for embellishing a city irrationally, it would seem a very natural venture for a group among whom André Breton had demonstrated his sensitivity to the Parisian environment, in *Nadja,* just as Louis Aragon had done in his *Le Paysan de Paris* (1926). Yet it is a different experiment altogether that most clearly reveals how the surrealists approached their "Recherches expérimentales" with very positive ambitions in the forefront of their minds. Setting out on February 11 to examine "the irrational possibilities of penetration and orientation in a picture," they chose Giorgio de Chirico's canvas *L'Enigme d'une journée,* which previously had belonged to Paul Eluard for a period of no less than a dozen years.

Eluard leaves no doubt on one score, when speaking about that particular experiment. He makes it perfectly clear that intentionality framed the questions posed on the subject of de Chirico's painting: "We had, drafting the questionnaire, the wish to make the atmosphere fantastic in that square where it seemed that nothing was to happen. We wanted, getting into that picture, to bring back to life everything that seemed to have come to a halt for good at a particularly empty moment in life." This clear statement of intent is offset puzzlingly by the further comment: "Everything accompanies man, but he runs a risk in letting the products of his imagination operate. It is possible that one day we shall be tempted for example to let ourselves live in a still life, to lay the foundations of our hopes and despair in the flank of a petal, a leaf or a fruit. No one will understand any more the reasons for our unreason and will call them dementia." Eluard has done no more than bring us back, now, to our point of departure. We still do not know how the whole experiment is to be conducted so as to produce desired results. How convincing can those results be, when achieved under unspecified controls, exercised not by irrational forces but by rational impulse?

The mode of experimental research described by Eluard presents disconcerting features pointing straight to the central ambition shared by those who joined in the games he discusses. This ambition grows out of the debatable but revealing assumption that one may advance from the rational to the irrational, at will and under controlled conditions ensuring elimination of the retarding influence of reason. It is in this sense that those activities termed here, for convenience, ludic are in fact serious modes of investigation, inquiries into forms of cognition. Having agreed to give their attention to an object selected by common consent, participants all share the same rational point of departure. Each of them makes an effort to move out from that base in pursuit of the irrational, deliberately employing means that seem to promise furthering their common ends: suppressing logical association, reacting as spontaneously as circumstances and mental capabilities allow. Then all return to base in order to review findings together, the wish and effort to do so giving real meaning to the words "inquiry" and "experimentation" that figure in Eluard's final report. In short, experimental research aimed at the conquest of irrational knowledge is not meant to induce even one player to go out of his head, but to give rational minds the impression of having explored the irrational.

How can we look insane, Eluard evidently implies, unless we *know* we look insane? In the venture on which he and his fellow surrealists embarked in 1933, the unencumbered spontaneity of the truly deranged mind was not only denied but actually would have taken participants out of their field of inquiry.

The more closely we examine the investigation called "Recherches expérimentales" and the findings it yielded in 1933, tbe more questionable the word "irrational" starts to appear, when applied to the kind of knowledge attained by participants. Faced with one leading question about the piece of pink velvet—"Of what sickness does it make one think?"—André Breton, René Char, and Georges Wenstein all replied, "Hysteria." As for Alberto Giacometti, his response was "Dementia praecox." We can only guess at the power of suggestion that may have induced three players out of a total of twelve to formulate the very same answer and led a fourth to a related response. However, two things are noticeable immediately. First, velvet (of whatever color) having no natural or agreed connection in people's minds with any form of sickness, the question posed was of a kind to solicit spontaneous association of an unpredictable character. Second, while quite independent of logical association, the reply given by one third of the participants borrowed the language of the world of reason to allude to a condition judged abnormal by society's standards of behavior. Giacometti's answer, especially, underlined most emphatically that respondents readily availed themselves of terminology by which those whose rationality is not in doubt habitually classify the state of certain individuals whose mental processes depart from the norm. Significantly, all four of the respondents cited looked toward the irrational, but from the safe vantage point of rationality. Doing so, they invited those to whom they knew in advance that their reply would be read aloud to look in the same direction, and from the same standpoint.

It may be argued that selection of just four answers out of twelve and concentration on but one question out of twenty-four can lead only to a crudely distorted interpretation of the scope and achievement of the surrealists' experiment with pink velvet. Other responses to the same question obviously stimulate the imagination more, Roger Caillois's "Dropsy," for example, Paul Eluard's "a lupus," and Benjamin Péret's "galoping consumption." The surprise released in us by these unforeseen answers sets off to advantage the benefits of joining in experimental re-

search into irrational knowledge. All the same, it tends to divert attention from the self-conscious nature of the surrealists' investigation.

On the one side may be grouped questions to which no totally
rational answer can be expected. These are questions by which the battle
against reason and in support of the irrational is half won even before
the first skirmish occurs. Is a piece of pink velvet diurnal or nocturnal?
How does it die? In what district of Paris does it live? What would be its
profession? Is it happy or unhappy? What language does it speak? The
strictly rational mind is quite incapable of addressing questions like
these, which in any case it treats as impertinent. Agreeing to attempt a
response is already an indication that certain individuals are willing to go
beyond the bounds of reason, even if it does not necessarily prove their
ability to do so.

On the other side are questions, far less numerous incidentally,
deliberately chosen so as to solicit, beyond the realm of reason, associations of a provocative kind. Not especially meaningful to an outsider
during the thirties, or even quite comprehensible to him, such questions were calculated to trigger specific sorts of responses in members of
the surrealist group. What should a piece of pink velvet meet on a
dissecting table, in order to create beauty? The purpose behind this
cryptic question was to evoke an image—"Beautiful as the chance encounter on a dissecting table of a sewing machine and an umbrella,"
from Lautréamont's *Les Chants de Maldoror*—that has always held the
surrealists' admiration as a perfect example of convulsive beauty, attained through words and in contempt of inherited aesthetic values.
There can be no doubt that participants acted under direct stimulus
from Lautréamont, rather than with total spontaneity, when formulating
replies among which stand out René Char's ("a cruiser on the hands of
mutineers"), Maurice Henry's ("gears, ten centimeters in diameter, cov-
ered in oil"), and Benjamin Péret's ("a moustache").

Raised again in connection with the clairvoyant's crystal ball, the
same question, "inspired by Lautréamont's image of genius," in Eluard's
phrase, prompted thoughts of surgery, anatomy, and death, elicited
apparently (this, at least, is Eluard's view) by association with the dissecting table, which he sees as influencing also the following question,
similarly inspired by Lautréamont: "What are the two objects with which
one would like to see it in a desert?" When we look down the list of
answers offered to these two leading questions we are struck by the
number of gaps, the frequency with which replies were deemed unwor-
thy of recording or reporting and with which respondents failed to reach

the standard set—as they were all keenly aware—in *Les Chants de Maldoror*. One of Eluard's published remarks brings to light something that merits emphasis here.

The last question posed with respect to the crystal ball is, "To what violation does it correspond?" After commenting methodically on the proceeding questions and on the responses engendered by them, Eluard appears to have only one thing to say upon reaching this one: "The word violation was not, in general, understood." The brevity of his observation intimates very clearly that, in his estimation, acceptable reaction to the question raised presupposed full comprehension of the word "violation." An error in semantics evidently invalidated several of the replies, in Eluard's eyes.

One can understand that Paul Eluard might have been disappointed with the effect of misunderstanding on the answers phrased by some respondents. However, his outright dismissal of those replies embodies a value judgment. It shows him looking for a connection between question and answer that rational thinking is fully capable of detecting. Could not an entirely irrelevant response probe the irrational with perfect success? This question comes to mind as we read a comment in Eluard's general introduction to his "Remarques." Here we are informed, "The only shortcoming with which one could reproach these automatic, quick responses is not rejecting certain free associations, either of ideas or sounds occurring sometimes between them and making them too interdependent. Certain elements in the response no longer apply to the question except in terms of similar elements or those closely linked with a preceding response" (pp. 19–20). How does that defect stand out, except when one makes a comparison between this or that individual's answers? Identifying it calls for an a posteriori judgment, detecting a weakness where the irrational mind would not be capable of noting one or would be indifferent to doing so. What are the acceptable limits, then? When do answers become not merely interdependent but too much so? Questions like these, meaningless to the insane, can be faced only by someone who retains a set of values, formulated and entertained by rational thinking. Moreover, the only way to avoid the defect condemned by Eluard is to engage in conscious censorship of one's replies to a questionnaire which, according to the rules of the game, ought to be answered with completely uninhibited spontaneity.

Oddly enough, asking "how you would kill" a piece of pink velvet brought in rather mundane responses, more practical, so to speak, than imaginative. Breton and Wenstein both would stamp on it. Char and Giacometti would rather knife it. César Moro and Tristan Tzara would shoot it, the former with a revolver, the latter with an archer's bow. Paul Eluard (who could suggest nothing more inventive than kicking the thing to death) reserves his approval for "the only irrational method" of disposing of velvet: intravenous injection, suggested by Jules Monnerot. One might argue that Péret comes close, when recommending stabbing in the heart. But challenging Eluard's choice is not our concern. What matters is the evaluative nature of comments to be found at this stage among his "Remarques." More especially, it is the basis on which evaluation is formulated.

Asking what that basis might be, we find the word "irrational" promoting confusion. The irrational is contrary to reason, of course. However, it denotes lack, the absence of reason. Hence it marks a flawed condition, falling short of the standard set by rationality. All the replies Eluard greeted with enthusiasm could be said to fall into this category, doing so largely because of the nature of the question to which they respond. The only one he salutes as proposing a truly irrational way of eliminating a piece of pink velvet is not simply irrational, though. It actually is antirational, for the adjective "antirational" identifies something actively defying reason, instead of just falling short of reason's demands. The all-important prefix indicates not only hostility toward reason, but counteraction; not only opposition, but neutralization.

Whereas irrational effect indeed may be achieved quite spontaneously, the antirational can come only by deliberate intent, expressing voluntary denial of reason's demands. We see this plainly when transferring our attention from the experiment centered on velvet to that devoted to "certain possibilities for irrational embellishment of a city."

The question asked about a selection of buildings and statues located in Paris was the following. Should they be preserved, relocated, modified, transformed or eliminated? Listed in haphazard order, thirty-one monuments ranged from obvious choices (the first was the Arc de Triomphe) to obscure ones (the last was the statue of Camille Desmoulins, executed in 1794 for protesting against the Terror). They featured tourists' preferences like the Obelisk, the Eiffel Tower, and the Sacré-Cœur, as well as monuments at which no sightseer would look twice (the statue of Chiappe and one of the railroad stations in the French capital, the Gare de l'Est). They included just one feature of the Parisian landscape that has always held a peculiar charm for surrealists, the enigmatic Saint-Jacques Tower. Thus the selection would be guaranteed to challenge respondents, to invite a variety of reactions, from admiration to derision—the statue of Clemenceau and that of Alfred de Musset making no more claim upon a surrealist's respect than the Invalides, Notre-Dame or the Panthéon.

Nowhere quite so clearly as in their suggestions for the irrational embellishment of Paris did those who participated in "experimental research" reveal their motivation and its effect on their responses. Nowhere quite so openly does Eluard display the criteria by which answers were chosen for publication:

> Sincere partisans of improvement, we have tried to embellish a little, physically and morally, the physiognomy of Paris, on which so many cadavers have left their imprint.
>
>   Let us congratulate ourselves on the excellence of the transformations effected. Some of them [he goes on to list a dozen examples] . . . can be, without false modesty, set as examples to architects and sculptors of good faith. (p. 23)

Eluard's self-congratulatory enthusiasm is proof we have left the zone of disinterested irrationalism and entered that of aggressive antirational activity, fired by dissatisfaction with the kinds of buildings and statues urban dwellers erect, according to Eluard, in an attempt to combat agoraphobia: "The monuments are either forsaken, stupid, useless or dedicated to the most insignificant superstitions, to the worst tasks. Rare exceptions apart, their ugliness appalls, stupefies, disfigures anyone who contemplates them. The statues, almost always of laughable, baneful individuals, are on plinths, which takes away any possibility of their intervening in human affairs and vice versa."

Eluard writes at this stage as though wishing to summarize the discussions that preceded selection of features of the Parisian landscape for much-needed improvement. Certainly, his remarks capture the spirit in which suggestions for embellishment were made on March 12, 1933. If proof of spontaneity is the haphazard, which confers a hit-or-miss character on purely automatic answers, then few of the replies Eluard retained for *Le Surréalisme au service de la Révolution* can be called unimpeachably spontaneous. The majority of them pointedly ridiculed this monument or that statue, in ways evidencing not only wilful rejection of its symbolic value (betraying deliberate resistance to its appeal) but also firm determination to discredit and even undermine it by means of a charge of subversive humor, laid at its foundation.

Paul Eluard's own recommendation was that the Arc de Triomphe be placed on its side, to become the best men's urinal in France. He proposed placing "a gilded turd" on the head of Joan of Arc's statue and a crudely sculpted phallus in its mouth. Maurice Henry would add a false beard and replace the national heroine's horse with an enormous hog. Meanwhile he and André Breton suggested very similar treatment for the statue marking the 1870 defense of Paris: Breton would add a matching ball and hairs; Henry would transform it into an enormous sex organ, the ball being one of its testicles, the phallus horizontal. Painted black and transported to the agricultural area of the Beauce, to the south of the French capital, at Breton's suggestion the Sacré-Cœur would become a tramway depot. Eluard proposed placing a deep-sea diver on the back of the statue known as the Lion of Belfort. In the diver's right hand would be a pot in which a hen was soaking. To Henry, the Paris Opera would look better transformed into a national academy for roller skating, admitting only nude women. Tristan Tzara saw it, rather, as housing the monkey and kangaroo sections of the Paris zoological garden. It would be set among skeletons, with a steel reproduction of a bicycle, as tall as the front of the building, standing on the steps. Tzara would like to fill the Sainte-Chapelle with sawdust. Breton would replace the car with a bathtub on the statue of automobile manufacturer Panhard. Benjamin Péret's recommendation for the same monument reads, "Transform it into a potato with the feet of a musketeer. The whole thing in a subway station," not far, we may suppose, from the statue of Camille Desmoulin, installed there, upon Eluard's recommendation, to punch tickets and close the gate to the platform.

To embellish Musset's statue, Eluard proposed an addition. Facing it he would erect a statue of "a vigorous exhibitionist, visibly charmed by the muse." Harfaux, on the other hand, required the whole statue to be painted in natural hues, removal of the plinth, and placement next to a cop, nude except for cap and nightstick. Maurice Henry would prefer simply seeing Alfred de Musset and his famous muse "on a bench, in 69 position." Tzara demanded that thousands of bronze sheep, plus one in Camembert cheese, be arranged around the statue of Clemenceau. Henry would be willing to retain the Panthéon untouched, on condition its name were changed to "Pantalon" (pants), and it be left perfectly empty. This would not satisfy Tristan Tzara, who called for slicing the monument dedicated to great men of the past and moving the two halves eighteen inches apart.

Destructive proposals were frequent, the first time the game was played. Breton demanded elimination of the statue of Gambetta. Both he and Wenstein wished to tear down the buildings surrounding the mysterious Saint-Jacques Tower. Eluard wanted Clemenceau's statue thrown out with the garbage.

Such recommendations usually came, however, with complementary suggestions. Calling for destruction of the monument to Clemenceau, Péret indicated that it should be replaced by "one of the golden pisshouses about which Lenin speaks." Eluard asked that the Vendôme Column be destroyed, on condition that it was torn down during a ceremony carefully repeating the one that destroyed it in 1871. Maurice Henry advised suppression of the statue of the Republic on the Place de la République, demanding that it be replaced by a statue to one of surrealism's heroes, the Marquis de Sade. Breton asked that the law courts, the Palais de Justice, be razed to the ground and replaced by a magnificent graffito, to be viewed from the air. To Wenstein it seemed that the Invalides, which houses the Old Soldiers' Home, the Army Museum, and Napoelon's Tomb, ought to be razed. The golden dome over the Tomb could then be set in a garden, surmounted by a bronze cast representing a motorcyclist experiencing the greatest difficulty inflating a tire.

Taking another look at the list of buildings and statues about which the surrealists asked their questions, we are struck by the extreme banality of those features of the Parisian landscape. The Saint-Jacques Tower stands alone in its appeal to the surrealist imagination. While the Passage de l'Opéra—evoked with such enthusiasm in Louis Aragon's *Le Paysan de Paris*—had to be left off the list, because it no longer existed after 1930, one wonders about the exclusion of the statue of Etienne Dolet, on the Place Maubert, which André Breton tells us in *Nadja* (where a photograph of it appears) both attracted and disturbed him. And what about the "very beautiful and very useless Porte Saint-Denis," also photographed for *Nadja*?

Such unexpected omissions are worth noting in connection with the unusually high percentage of suppressed answers (or of blanks on the answer sheets), in the report on surrealist recommendations for embellishing Paris. Paul Eluard's total of published responses runs to no more than seventeen. As for Benjamin Péret, the surrealist automatist *par excellence*, only ten of his replies to thirty-one questions appear in print. Retention of just a limited number of answers indicates how few of them survived self-censorship and a rigorous selective process. The evidence set out in *Le Surréalisme au service de la Révolution* leads to the conclusion that selection was not made specifically to demonstrate how many surrealists had managed to close the gap between the rational and the irrational. Instead, choices were shared with the public as proof of imagination's ability to challenge reasonable expectation. Formulating such a challenge and seeing it through meant being fully cognizant of and firmly opposed to the utilitarian function of the monument to be modified and of the significance of the statue to be transformed. Thus it was the rational that set the norm by which the originality of all proposals was evaluated, even when the irrational offered a standard by which those proposals could be measured.

The investigation devised to embellish Paris and the one centered on a painting are related. Each takes its point of departure in a purposeful spirit of experimentation, "the wish to make the atmosphere fantastic" in a de Chirico coming from the same source as that which, according to Paul Eluard, led participants to try to "embellish a little . . . the physiognomy of Paris." Antirational motivation is discernible in both forms of inquiry. Nevertheless, they still differ to a noteworthy degree. It is the experiment with the painting that in the end deserves to be acknowledged as the more disinterested. The one concerned with the French capital reveals more about the range, scope, and orientation of the surrealists' "experimental research."

The answers about de Chirico's *L'Enigme d'une journée* are more numerous than on any other questionnaire, especially the one about Paris. Examination of the replies shows that nine, for sure, of the eleven participants (including Eluard and Péret) responded to all fifteen questions. Evidently, this questionnaire was of a nature to solicit, very successfully indeed, many relatively extensive answers that contrast with the brief replies often set down during other inquiries.

Looking into the questions asked, we discover that, by and large, they tended to direct the respondent's attention inward, the painting being used to focus imaginative effort and to give it clear direction. In other words, the whole experiment required participants to look to de Chirico's canvas for imaginative stimulus, by posing questions devised to invite their contribution to elucidating the enigma the painter had contrived to render in pictorial terms.

Questions were of two kinds, essentially. One sort asked respondents to supply elements omitted or suppressed by de Chirico: "Where is the sea?" "Describe the countryside surrounding the town?" "Whom does the statue represent?" The other sort required each spectator to project himself into the picture, either speculatively ("Who will be the first person arriving on the square? Where will he or she come from? What will he or she be like? What will he or she be doing there?") or quite literally: "Arriving in the square, what will you go see first of all?" Both kinds of query encouraged entry into an enigmatic situation thanks to an imaginative effort, made beyond rational limitations quite inappropriate to the scene Giorgio de Chirico has depicted.

Two de Chirico drawings had been reproduced in the opening number (December 1, 1924) of *La Révolution surréaliste,* where the very first text was the transcription of one of his dreams. His work had been represented in the first surrealist group exhibition in November 1925 and discussed by André Breton in the course of a series of articles from which came the first edition (1928) of *Le Surréalisme et la peinture,* the pioneering essay on surrealism and painting. A de Chirico seems to have looked an ideal choice for the sort of inquiry that provided the occasion in 1933 for surrealist experimental research into pictorial imagery. The essential feature of *L'Enigme d'une journée* after all, in the context of the investigation that held the surrealists' curiosity, was the way the canvas so fruitfully offered a focal point for the kind of imaginative play that those who joined in—all fervent admirers of Giorgio de Chirico—were eager to explore. By contrast, some of the monuments on which they agreed to concentrate, in a parallel experiment, seem ludicrously unlikely choices.

The group activity directed in March of 1933 at imaginative embellishment of Paris retains its ludic character, naturally. However, comparison with the investigation centered on *L'Enigme d'une journée* suggests a fundamentally serious wager, this time. Mostly, those involved were working with basically unpromising material. They were attempting to estimate the liberative power of man's imagination by reference to familiar features of the urban landscape which they regarded as not merely unattractive and quite unexciting but as positively offensive or at least entirely depressing. To surrealist eyes, these monuments, whether public buildings or statues to personalities from the past, are distinguished only by their utter banality and their revolting symbolic value, oppressively representative of reactionary forces that surrealists, to a man, view as weighing down modern life: church, state, army, industrialism, inferior poetry, and so on.

For a brief miraculous period just after the turn of the century, Giorgio de Chirico had maintained with inexplicable consistency a level of luminous creativity that surrealists everywhere salute as marvelously poetic. Hence, in their estimation almost any early canvas by the Italian painter might have served the same stimulative purpose as *L'Enigme d'une journée.* On the other hand, the great majority of monuments chosen for treatment during the process of embellishing Paris irrationally were selected, it appears, not so much because they were in urgent need of modification or replacement as because they were, by surrealist standards, profoundly antipoetic phenomena, marring the urban scene.

This then is the value of the two complementary experiments, approaching reality from diametrically opposed extremes. The questions posed on the subject of *L'Enigme d'une journée* guaranteed total freedom by letting the imagination run at will. On the other hand, the topography of one of the world's great cities was to be modified by purposeful imaginative action. Directed inward, as each participant contemplated de Chirico's canvas, imaginative play afforded him the chance to learn more about himself. Directed outward toward monuments for which he felt neither respect nor affection, imagination fulfilled the other essential function reserved for it in surrealist poetic practice: it contributed directly to bringing about what Benjamin Péret once termed, with reference to poetry, "a rectification of the universe."

It goes without saying that the surrealists' imaginative suggestions for improving the appearance of the French capital marked a protest against common sense. More than this, though, they resisted domination of day-to-day living by banality and by social values to which surrealists never cease to be profoundly opposed. Participation in the experiment focused on Paris was proof of eagerness to change a situation that could be remedied, surrealists believe, only by stubborn opposition to a pervasive antipoetic spirit. Exercise of the imagination, at the expense of the designated function of monuments chosen for attention because they gave offense, was taken, in other words, for a responsible act of poetic significance.

Did that act, though, deserve the label that surrealists attached to it? Was it truly irrational in nature? When we consider the degree to which participants in the experiment engaged in conscious resistance, the extent to which their protest against the symbolism of the Invalides, Notre-Dame Cathedral, and so on reflected contempt or even anger, the validity of the term "irrational" becomes quite doubtful. Instead, we find them to have reacted against an impression of ugliness that—most of the time, any way—was not grounded in aesthetic sense (Etienne Dolet looks no better, in this respect, that Joan of Arc, and many would say he looks worse) but in moral values. Although, as the case of Breton's reaction to Dolet's statue reminds us, there are exceptions, by and large it is thought, not feeling, that underlies a surrealist's approval or disapproval as he looks at Parisian monuments. And it is thought that motivates him to propose changes in what he sees. So far as it is permissible to speak, as a surrealist would do, of the 1933 proposals for transforming the landscape of Paris as poetic in character, objectivity requires us to acknowledge that it is the antirational, not the irrational, that contributes to rectifying the universe.

Conclusion

WITH ANDRÉ BRETON at their head, those in the surrealist movement have the highest possible regard for poetry, looking upon it, just as Breton does, as "the perfect compensation for the miseries we endure." At the same time, all of them view reason and the rational process as able to fill only a secondary role—and a very limited one, at that—in solving problems of the life of the spirit.

This is demonstrated over and over again by the surrealists' persistent concern to master lucid exposition in the presentation of their ideas on poetry's central role in assisting man to come to terms with living in the modern world. Meanwhile, the distinction between images and logical propositions, to which Philippe Soupault has directed attention, explains Benjamin Péret's preeminence among surrealist writers. Péret's poems develop not out of ideas but of images that proliferate as they invade the printed page, beyond the control of logic and of what is commonly termed good sense. Thus the contrast could not be greater or more revealing between Péret's poems, the product of automatic writing, and the essays—second in importance, among those coming out of France, only to the articles by Breton himself—in which he comments on the function of poetry. Surrealist theory restricts the fruitful operation of reason very narrowly indeed. It grants rational processes of thought no more than the privilege of weighing, after the event, whatever poetic action has proved itself capable of bringing to light. In addition, it imposes on reason the attendant obligation to acknowledge that poetic revelation exceeds and can never be fully encompassed within rational projection.

To reason surrealists prefer imagination, said in Breton's first manifesto to be "perhaps on the point of reclaiming its rights." In surrealism, attention goes to "strange forces" lurking in "the depths of our minds" which, once "tapped," can be submitted, afterward, to reason's inspection, "if need be" (p. 23). At this point, despite Breton's respect for clarity in presentation of theoretical issues, his ideas become cloudy. The manifesto does not make clear what sort of need he has in mind, omitting to indicate how imperious it must be before inspection by reason becomes possible, is permissible or is required. Still, one thing stands out plainly in what Breton writes: "Reason is not enough." Surrealism may not have actually taken its point of departure in this lapidary statement. All the same, surrealists were not long discovering it stood like a signpost, indicating the route they must take, as they pressed forward in a direction that would lead them inevitably away from the accepted norms of early-twentieth-century poetry. The image appears vital and exciting, in surrealism, when it combats reasonable expectation. Hence surrealists respond most enthusiastically to images that deny reason the right to arbitrate, to classify, to judge authoritatively. The multivalence of words and forms (like those ambiguous, amorphous but precisely delineated shapes inhabiting Yves Tanguy's pictorial universe) is surrealism's riposte to reason's claims. It promotes reorientation of thought, as part of the reeducation of man's sensibility to which all surrealists are wholeheartedly dedicated.

If reason was to be stigmatized as insufficient, did not its absence hold out the promise of something never to be found in the reasonable? The question appeared logical to those who founded surrealism. It looked unavoidable, even, given their firm belief that, along the road to poetic revelation, rationality is nothing but an obstruction, slowing down progress when not bringing it altogether to a stop.

Turning from theory to practice, we at once find a prime virtue of the surrealists' adamant opposition to reason. It confronts a fear inculcated in poets by society's values, which engender suspicion about the usefulness of poetry, its practical utility. This is the fear of losing an audience, unless the products of the poetic imagination are dutifully brought before reason for approval and, accordingly, are adjusted at the moment of expression to requirements set by rational discourse. It is true, beyond a doubt, that only the weakest of poets—the least poetic, in short—regularly confuse poetic statements with strictly rational communication. All the same, even the best of them, it appeared to those rallying behind Breton, are open to the temptations of a conviction that strikes the surrealist mind as totally erroneous and quite pernicious. By and large, poets tend to subscribe without serious resistance to the view that sharing poetic intuition with others entails channeling uncommon poetic evidence through common sense. The surrealist argues, conversely, that the vital poetic message can only be harmed, or at the very least diluted, by submissive respect for reason, not only during the moment of gestation but also during the procedure allowing the poet to place his discovery before the public.

From all this the surrealists make a deduction of fundamental importance. They infer that the irrational may be, can be, and surely *is*, capable of nurturing poetic statements such as the rational can neither formulate nor suffice to convey. Their consequent deduction is that, in any field of creative endeavor, insanity has the ability to foster poetry of a kind that it would be quite impertinent of reason to attempt to regulate and evaluate. Examining this conclusion, we perceive that they have adopted a position seemingly more than a little paradoxical.

If surrealist poets have cause to admire the madman, to envy what he produces in the measure that he is not as the rest of us are, then should not their ambition be to know at first hand what it is to be insane? In fact, should they not admit in all honesty that those remaining sane are condemned by soundness of mind to be, at best, only second-rate poets? Logically persuasive up to a certain point, in the end these questions lose their relevance to the surrealist argument. A glance at the eleventh number of *La Révolution surréaliste* helps indicate why this happens.

In three of the six photographs borrowed from the Charcot archives that accompany the text commemorating "Le Cinquantenaire de l'hystérie," the patient is seen staring out of her cot at something not visible to us.[1] Two more photos show her lying with her eyes closed. Only in the last picture can the hysterical patient be seen gazing full into the camera. In five cases out of six, then, the subject photographed appears entirely unaware of the presence of the cameraman. Meanwhile the experience to which hysteria has opened up a pathway is one we are denied hope of sharing. The strangely dramatic body positions to which moments of hysteria may lead can be observed by all of us. But whatever emotion or thought or vision has induced this or that posture eludes us. What has provoked in one photo the ecstatic expression on the upturned face or the beatific smile in another, this time showing closed eyes? What has prompted the woman whose eyes we cannot see to thrust out her tongue? A vulgar thought? Or a lascivious one? These and other questions raised by the photographs must go unanswered. As the inadequacy of the evidence demonstrates unambiguously, no one can hope to share in something he is permitted to observe simply the way the camera does.

The fault does not lie by any means with still photography. Fascinating as it would be, a movie film would tell us only a limited amount more, even with sound. For the photographs illustrating "Les Attitudes passionnelles en 1878" can merely hint at the nature of the experiences imposed on some of Charcot's patients by their hysterical condition. Hence the documentation of hysteria provided in *La Révolution surréaliste* brings before us proof of our inability to bridge a gap that, by their very existence, those pieces of filmed evidence serve to actually broaden.

Although unrestrained by reason, the insane artist is not entirely free in the use he will make of his medium. What he eventually creates will have been imposed upon him by a mental state outside normalcy. The motivating energy of his art owes little or nothing to the impulse to reach others. The insane write or paint for themselves, under irresistible compulsion more often than out of a conscious desire to share their vision or ideas with an audience. So far as the insane artist finally reaches a public, he does so in a manner that brings to mind Charcot's patients, unaware and so unmindful of being immobilized by the camera in passional attitudes that stimulate other people's curiosity by their oddity. In these circumstances, profound appreciation is less likely to follow than a kind of voyeurism.

One might say, therefore, that someone who creates out of his madness is the embodiment of the alienated artist, about whose plight in the modern world we hear so much. However, the situation created by the existence of insane art is at once simpler and more complex than it sounds. For the spectacle of insanity places the observer in a predicament. If he seeks, for example with a camera, to make a record of what happens to those possessed by hysteria, he does no more in the final analysis than draw attention to the barrier separating the world called normal from the one that a general consensus authorizes calling abnormal. Yet it is not the observer who erects that barrier. However much he desires to see it removed, it will stand so long as mental disorder keeps the artists under study apart from the rest of mankind. How then is the barrier to be cast down, if not removed altogether? How can the public be enabled to step out of the world familiar to them, in order to join the artist who is looking another way, his eyes closed to everyday reality? How are they to be made to see what he is seeing with closed eyes?

Reviewing these and related questions, we see at once that it would be useless to expect answers to come from an artist who creates out of his madness. It is no less futile to pose those same questions to a specialist in disorders of the mind, who looks upon the work of a madman as proof of a condition and, possibly, a key to its cure. As for the surrealist, he cannot really help, either.

So long as a surrealist retains his sanity, he can approach and undertake to assess something produced by an insane artist only from the standpoint of an outsider, as a spectator whose position is radically different from that of the work's creator. He is free, naturally, to examine what he sees or reads in a manner that brings to light in it some form of oracular revelation or shows it to be illuminating in a way to which he finds himself particularly sensitive. All the same, just like André Breton in Nadja's company, he will contemplate what insanity has inspired without first having entered the state in which it originated and from where, for all *he* knows, it may look or sound rather different, perhaps radically so. In short, his basis for judgment is essentially the same as that of other people who, as the saying goes, have not lost their minds. The judgment he will make will be conditioned by his outlook as a surrealist, of course. Even so, what he gladly admires and terms revelation reaches him from beyond a barrier which he himself has not crossed and (luckily, he will confess, if perfectly honest) cannot pass so long as he retains his reason. In fact, a surrealist becomes aware of illumination and responds to revelation, in what insanity has brought to his notice, precisely because he remains safely on his own side of the barrier. There, it must be admitted, common sense helps put his hand on a yardstick. Without the latter, whatever the artist has placed before him could never be measured accurately on a scale calibrated by surrealist ambitions.

Philippe Audoin has gone to the trouble of stressing one feature of his fellow surrealists' attitude toward insanity, as exemplified in Breton's relationship with Nadja. He has denied that "surrealist thought . . . has had a taste for shipwreck."[2] Something more needs to be added, to make the surrealist position clearer. Surrealists have always been responsive to the attraction of Charles Baudelaire's injunction, captured in the graphic metaphor of plunging into the whirlpool to seek the new. To the surrealist, however, the new is not mere novelty but revelation. The nature of his admiration for Baudelaire's writings allows us to grasp that

he never ceases to be convinced that revelation comes only with searching.

Baudelaire's metaphor derives, we may guess, from the title and
central image of Edgar Allan Poe's story *A Descent into the Maelström*,
where we read, "After a little while I became possessed with the keenest
curiosity about the whirl itself. I positively felt a *wish* to explore its
depths, even at the sacrifice I was going to make; and my principal grief
was that I should never be able to tell my old companions on shore
about the mysteries I should see." Ever wary of shipwreck, of "plunging
headlong," as Poe expresses it, "at once and for ever, into the chaos of
the foam below," surrealists adopt a position that denotes reservations
about the value of art produced in a state of mental derangement.

Without for an instant concealing their indebtedness to a number
of artists for works nurtured by mental illness, surrealists recognize that
such works narrowly reflect the forms of obsession that have unbalanced
their creators' minds, closing them to all else. This, presumably, is why
surrealism ascribes special value to the accomplishments of certain insane artists while finding less or even nothing at all of interest in work
by others, just as free of reason's control.

Stransky's term "intrapsychic ataxia" is one that we can feel sure
has never passed a surrealist's lips. It identifies the dislocative effect of
schizophrenia, its negative, disruptive force, which Bleuler saw as the
reason not only why schizophrenic behavior is often contradictory and
marked by incongruousness but also why schizophrenic thought can be
chaotic and inconsequential. The reasons surrealists have never had
occasion to allude to intrapsychic ataxia are pertinent to comprehension
of their assessment of various forms of art reflecting mental disturbance.

When he criticized the surrealists for respecting the dictionary
instead of coining neologisms the way he thought they should, Gaston
Ferdière saw things quite out of true. In the surrealists' use of language
what really requires emphasis is their innate sense of order, evidenced
from the beginning in the rhythm and syntactical correctness of the first
surrealist automatic texts.[3] How else to explain the interest shown by
Breton and Eluard in training the mind poetically so that it can produce,
by intention, something that will pass for having been written in the
absence of control? Training (the substantive *l'entraînement* and the
verb *dresser* both occur in the introduction to "Les Possessions" in
L'Immaculée Conception), and not the loss of mental faculties, underlies
the "new exercise of thought" vigorously advocated by Breton and Eluard
when they recommended simulating insanity.

By the same token, it was not simply with the purpose of evoking obsession, of accepting its irresistible limitations as a fair price for illumination, that Breton and Ernst both spoke of hallucination. Max Ernst referred specifically to his own *powers* of hallucination, while Breton stipulated an activity not only hallucinatory but voluntarily so. Faithful in their thinking to surrealism's underlying principles, both equated the "spiritual hunt" to which Arthur Rimbaud had referred with a procedure he had termed "the derangement of all the senses." And, like Rimbaud, they insisted that derangement must be *reasoned*, if it is to be truly fruitful. Each in his own way, therefore, Ernst and Breton sought to make use of hallucination, to employ it as an instrument for investigating the surreal. When doing so, they demonstrated that a surrealist's abiding preoccupation with self-preservation embraces more than deep concern for continued maintenance of his mental stability.

Of course, it would be naive to discount elementary considerations. André Breton, whose right to leadership would never be challenged by any surrealist in France, was to remember all his life how frighteningly high a price is paid, psychologically and socially, by the mentally disturbed. There could never be any doubt where his influence would be brought to bear, should voluntary surrender of sanity be proposed as a fitting goal for surrealist endeavor. Easily enough taken for no more than a sign of caution tinged with lack of courage, his *wish* to retain a firm grip on his senses signifies more than compromise, however. In surrealist poetic practice, taking care not to be swallowed up in the whirlpool is a clear indication of the artist's determination to hold onto self-awareness. More than a safeguard of health, self-awareness is meant to guarantee him continued efficiency and integrity as a poet.

Illumination of what is involved comes, as it happens, less quickly from this or that pronouncement by Breton or one of his associates than from a brief remark by a psychiatrist, Dr. Anne Tholose: "Therefore we believe that any birth of communication, so long as it is an exchange, carries with it the risk of falling into Madness."[4] Although not intended for one moment to situate poetry with respect to productive exchange between men, this one sentence places in our hands the key without which we cannot unlock the door to surrealist poetry.

Since the most prominent among those who became surrealists were devoted to poetry before surrealism ever came into existence, there seems some excuse for passing over the significance of their admiring references to earlier poets, both during their initiation into surrealism and afterward. It is supremely important, though, that when seeking models by which to judge their own accomplishments, they found these primarily in nineteenth-century French and German writers and painters. Fascination with mental disturbance as a source of poetic stimulation (even as evidenced in the work of some admired predecessors) never really diverts the surrealists' attention from their main objective. First and last, they aim to evaluate their own efforts at communication by relating them to a revolutionary poetic tradition. Not one among them has ever made the mistake of attempting to measure his or her creative action beside that which society confidently dubs insane and hence quickly sets aside as extraneous to normal healthy life. Before anything else, doing such a thing would be a major tactical error in an authentic representative of a group that insists at all times on being judged as persistently occupied with the central concerns of modern living.

The limits prudently set upon exploration of the hallucinatory state in the interest of surrealist inquiry explain why, in "Le Cinquantenaire de l'hystérie," Louis Aragon and André Breton refrained from giving the noun "hysteria" the force it once had in pathology. As "a supreme means of expression," hysteria appears as, essentially, a mode of communication available to the true poet. Whereas Aragon and Breton stopped short of drawing up a statement to define hysteria, as viewed from the surrealist standpoint, they unhesitatingly labeled it none the less a "poetic discovery." Thus they indicated in which area of human activity it held vital meaning for them and for those whose opinions they were putting into words when celebrating the fiftieth anniversary of Charcot's experiments. Like hallucination, hysteria had come to denote in surrealism a reliable poetic instrument, rather than a regrettably deficient mental condition.

All this should not lead us to suppose every surrealist bent at all cost on persuading others that mental stress necessarily diminishes artistic achievement. Such an inference would make nonsense of the surrealists' public expression of deep admiration for individual artists whose work is enriched by a vision that comes only when sanity has gone. All the same, the advantages stand out, when one contrasts with a mentally disturbed artist the creative surrealist who has succeeded in attaining one of his poetic ideals: entering and leaving a state of hallucination entirely at will.

The insane artist is not merely in danger of being deprived of liberty, because social prejudice holds the threat of confinement to a mental institution over the heads of all whose conduct does not conform in prescribed ways. He or she has lost, surrendered or been deprived of the privilege of enjoying from choice a viewpoint that, so surrealism teaches, the sane artist can come very close to sharing voluntarily.

Breton's cautious regulation of his own experiments with hallucination, via automatic writing, was not motivated exclusively by the wish to safeguard his mental health. It betrayed just as significantly his need to dominate poetic expression and to be able to enjoy the benefits of poetic vision when and as he elected to sample them.

The need just mentioned relates to the paramount concern of all who follow Breton's lead. On its first page the second surrealist manifesto refers to surrealism as tending to provoke "a *crisis of consciousness* of the most general and most serious kind." This is a critically important statement, one we find illuminated if we examine some photographic evidence of a sort quite different from that preserved in the Charcot archives.

On the cover of the seventh number of *La Révolution surréaliste* (June 15, 1926) appeared a photograph captioned "The Last [Most Recent] Conversions." It showed a group of people in a Paris street (the Juillet Column is visible in the background), all looking up in the same direction, either shading their eyes with their hands or gazing through smoked glass. The photo was taken by Eugène Atget, whose work had attracted the notice of a neighbor, Man Ray, who had brought it to the attention of his fellow surrealists in France. It was published anonymously, as were all the photographs by Atget used in the first surrealist magazine. Presumably this was at the request of the photographer,[5] whom we cannot credit, however, with assigning the title it bears.

Use of smoked glass by several spectators does suggest that all present must be watching a solar eclipse. Even so, in the top left-hand corner of the print is a dark shadowed area at which everyone seems to be staring intently. According to one commentator, this gives the impression that "some two dozen people are looking through virtually opaque glass to see what will appear to be a black sun."[6] But how can this be? The edge of the shaded zone nearest the crowd is concave, not convex as one would expect the blackened sun to be. Moreover, easy enough to ignore because no one in frame is looking at it, there is a hint of a corresponding but reversed shadow—a second sun?—at the top right of the picture.

Accepting the shaded area as indeed a black or blacked-out sun means believing the sun has come to within a few feet of the ground. So then, logically, it would have liquified the camera and photographic plate (to say nothing of the audience and Atget himself) before the photograph could be taken. Giving up the theory that the shadowy zone is to be interpreted as a distorted sun in eclipse leaves us to entertain a more reasonable hypothesis. However, if we go on to conclude that the shot was taken from within a tunnel, whose presence intrudes distractingly upon the scene, we face the obligation to answer an unsettling question: Where could such a tunnel be located?

In Berenice Abbott's collection, *20 Photographs by Eugène Atget, 1856–1927*, the upper left shadow has been dodged out. Abbott's solution is certainly practical. It has invested one of Atget's works with unquestionable documentary value; but at what price! One wonders what Abbott would have done with Atget's photograph of the Austrian Embassy or with his picture titled *Coiffeur, Avenue de l'Observatoire* (c. 1923). Any way, dodging out is only an attempt to dodge the issue.

What makes us accept the idea that the knot of people in one photograph are all attentively watching an eclipse is not merely the persuasive clue provided by the smoked glass some are holding in front of their eyes. It is, even more compellingly, the perplexity to which we would be committed if we thought something other than an eclipse had caused them all to stop and stare long enough for Atget to set up his cumbersome equipment and shoot.

We know of course that Jean-Eugène-Auguste Atget saw himself as a documentary photographer and that of the thousands of prints he left behind upon his death in 1927, at the age of seventy, Man Ray found less than fifty to be worth acquiring. Also, it would be foolish to ignore the warning implicit in Ray's comment, "I don't want to make any mystery out of Atget at all. He was a simple man and he was using the material that was available to him when he started around 1900. An old rickety camera with a brass lens on it and a cap. He's just take the cap off and put it back."[7] Atget was interested in recording curiosities observable in the world about him. The second issue of *La Révolution surréaliste* (15 January 1925) carried his picture of a bald man in a circus wagon, thrusting his head between the jaws of an alligator which he has pried open. In the seventh number appeared a photograph of a corset shop, which supposedly took Atget's attention because near the doorway hung a corseted but headless tailor's dummy, suspended outside above a half-skirt animated by the breeze.

All this being said, two indisputable facts remain and cannot be ignored. In order to eliminate the distracting shadows and to concentrate attention on the documentary force of his picture, Atget might quite simply have cropped the print of the eclipse-watching crowd. Nevertheless, instead of doing so, without retouching it he permitted the surrealists to publish it.

Now it is possible that of the photographs preserved in the Salpêtrière Hospital those in which some of Charcot's patients seem to be
gazing at something invisible owe their strange effect to cropping. Even
so, it appears quite unlikely that the unidentified photographer would
have wilfully denied us the opportunity to see what is in front of these
women. Such conduct, we must all agree, would conflict unpardonably
with the documentary nature of the evidence he had been hired to
compile in the interest of medical science. On the other hand, the
absence of any proof to the contrary allows us to attribute the strange
interposition of extraneous shadow in Atget's Paris street scene to nothing other than the unforeseen vignetting effect of the camera's lens
barrel. Hence it is both accidental and unavoidable at the same time.
And this is the very reason why the uncropped, unmodified print is
granted pride of place on the front cover of an issue of *La Révolution
surréaliste*.

This is not to say, by any means, that Eugène Atget was a surrealist
photographer. In one of his letters, written in 1955, Man Ray states
most equitably, "The blurred figures were not intentional, any more
than the reflections in the window."[8] Yet these and other accidental
features caught by Atget's camera introduce into his pictures the element
of *l'insolite* (the unwonted) and *le merveilleux* (the marvelous) so dear to
all surrealists. In relation to the latter's love of the mannequin,[9] accidental (and again unavoidable) superimposition on the corseted dummies
visible in the shop window of *Corsets* of disconnected words like "A.
SIMON," "OUVERT," "DIMANCHE," "DEMANDEZ," and "CATALOGUE IL-
LUSTRÉ," painted on the transparent storefront glass are especially worthy of mention. Just as noteworthy is the mysterious repetition of the
numeral 5 in *Cabaret*, a photograph belonging to a series about Paris
brothels which Atget was commissioned to execute for a book on pros-
titution. In a shot of a newsstand, what impresses above all is a broad-
sheet for the daily *Le Matin*, blurred by a breeze that has left only its
headline legible: "SABOTAGE À LA DYNAMITE."

Surrealists delight in enticing their audience into accompanying
them down a path along which—like a compass that unaccountably has
gone awry—reason soon has ceased to be of use in any effort to check
our bearings. Our surrealist guides now permit us to observe that we
can emerge from the unfamiliar situation into which they have led us
(more precisely, come to terms with it) only when, giving up relying
on reason, we look to imagination for assistance. Thus following Luis
Buñuel's film *Un Chien andalou*, for instance, we become witnesses to
the failure of the rational deductive process, which proves incapable of

making sense of successive filmed sequences (in which we look in vain for narrative progress) and of the images featured in them. Imagination, surrealist creative action demonstrates, is the only means by which one can go on advancing in the light cast by the poetic work. Moving forward, we have occasion to acknowledge one fact over and over again. In the surrealist poetic experience, reason is granted a small role; but not a negligible one. It is assigned a controlled part in bringing the marvelous to the surface of consciousness. Denied full satisfaction while still aspiring to reach it, reason is confronted with its own inadequacies. And it is at the crucial point where reason has to admit its own inability to explain and to account for what we see or hear that imagination intervenes, reclaiming the rights reserved for it no later than the first surrealist manifesto.

There can be no doubt that all surrealists gladly would ascribe the manifestation of many of the elements fascinating them in Atget's photographs to the welcome and inexplicable intervention of beneficent chance. Every one of them sees the latter as operating against the limitations that reason tries to impose upon our response to reality and hence directly against the documentary purpose Eugène Atget had made his own before he ever met Ray. But there is no doubt, either, that, eagerly responsive to the unpredictable effects of chance, the surrealist sensibility places upon these an interpretation wholly consistent with surrealism's energetic devotion to the task of provoking a crisis of consciousness to which André Breton alluded in his second manifesto. Something very similar may be said about the surrealists' reaction to the work of some insane artists.

It is solely the liberative effect of mental derangement, as made concrete in the imagery presented by certain insane artists, that the surrealist prizes. Insanity appeals to him only when and as it frees verbal and pictorial expression from unwelcome rational restraints that he deprecates as anti-poetic in essence. Surrealists may aim to emulate the results that insanity can bring, but do not intend to shut themselves up in the state of mind that has bred these results. Consistently and unceasingly, they go on proclaiming the virtues of holding rationality in check. They do not advocate, though, surrendering it altogether, once and for all, lest incoherence defuse the poetic statement, denying it imaginative appeal by incautiously divesting it of the precious quality of communicability. In the circumstances, surrealist experimentation that simulates insanity is not indicative of halfheartedness, of prudent compromise, open to criticism or meriting suspicion. It denotes, on the contrary, a serious effort to resolve the conflict between reason and unreason, in terms that offer surrealist creative artists the prospect of attaining the poetic beyond the reach of reason's dictatorship, but also without temporary or permanent surrender to insanity. Thus manifestation of anti-rational intent, during the period of "experimental research" occurring in 1933, was entirely consistent with the surrealists' wish, dating back to the first manifesto of 1924, to assign the reasoning mind the limited but necessary role of spectator, of witness to imagination's revelations.

During moments of surrealist poetic activity, imagination operates with a freedom that develops best while reason is subject to restraint. At the moment when the process of poetic communication finds completion, though, when an audience is invited to share the artist's discovery, reason is permitted a distinctly more positive role. To the surrealist that role appears valuable in the measure that it serves the cause of poetry by letting reason testify to the true character of surrealist imagery. Reason's function, now, is to acknowledge the essentially disruptive nature of the surrealist poetic image. Thus reason has played its part when it has contributed to showing that, dislocating the sense of continuity thanks to which we habitually recognize and accept everyday reality, poetry offers evidence of a higher reality called surreality.

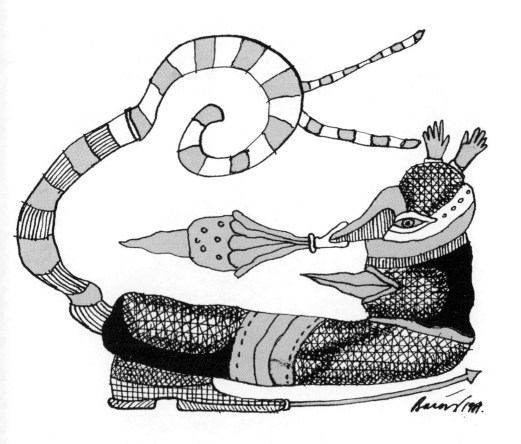

$\mathcal{N}otes$

Unless otherwise indicated, the place of publication for all books in French is Paris.

CHAPTER 1—SURREALISM AND PSYCHOSIS

1. J. Garrabé, "Prolégomènes à un manifeste de la surpsychiatrie," *L'Evolution psychiatrique* 44, no. 1 (January–March 1979):15.

2. Jean Broustra, "Osiris est un dieu noir," *L'Evolution psychiatrique* 44, no. 1 (January–March 1979):63.

3. Adolfo Fernandez Zoïla, "Mots en jeu/en jeu de mots," *L'Evolution psychiatrique* 44, no. 1 (January–March 1979):34.

4. Maurice Blanchot, "Réflexions sur le surréalisme," in his *La Part du feu* (Gallimard, 1949), p. 91.

5. Leonora Carrington's text first appeared in English as "Down Below," in the fourth number of the American surrealist magazine *VVV* (February 1944). The French text was published by Editions Fontaine in 1945. The English version was reissued in 1975 as the fifth in the "Surrealist Research & Development Monograph" Series, published by *Radical America* under the direction of the Surrealist Group in Chicago.

6. J.-L. Armand-Laroche, "Les Surréalistes, l'inconscient et Antonin Artaud," *L'Evolution psychiatrique* 44, no. 1 (January–March 1979):100.

7. André Breton, *Second Manifeste du surréalisme*, in his *Manifestes du surréalisme* [Jean-Jacques Pauvert, n. d. (1962)], p. 191.

CHAPTER 2—INTRODUCTION TO PSYCHIATRY

1. "Lettre aux Médecins-chefs des asiles de fous," *La Révolution surréaliste* 3 (15 April 1925):29. Artaud was to return to his attack on psychiatrists in an essay, "L'Osselet toxique," printed in the eleventh number (15 March 1928) of *La Révolution surréaliste*, p. 12.

2. André Breton, *Entretiens* (Gallimard, 1952), p. 29.

3. André Breton, *Nadja* (1928), revised edition (Gallimard, 1962), p. 44. All subsequent parenthetical page references are to this revised edition.

A lengthy section of *Nadja* is devoted to summarizing *Les Détraquées*, the only stage play, Breton assures his readers, that he cares to remember. Breton had already expressed his gratitude to Babinski in his 1924 surrealist manifesto.

4. Lucien Bonnafé, "La Leçon surréaliste," *L'Evolution psychiatrique* 44, no. 1 (January–March 1979):48. A description of the *IVe fiévreux* is to be found in René R. Held, *L'Œil du psychanalyste* (Payot, 1973).

5. André Breton, *Manifestes du surréalisme*, pp. 36–37. In a letter to Tristan Tzara dated April 4, 1919, Breton wrote, "I have done little philosophy: a class in high school and a few readings but psychiatry is very familiar to me (I am a medical student, although less and less so). Kräpelin and Freud have caused me very big excitement." See Michel Sanouillet, *Dada à Paris* (Jean-Jacques Pauvert, 1965), pp. 443–44.

An evaluation of surrealist automatic writing from the medical standpoint is provided in Jean Cazaux, *Surréalisme et psychologie: endophasie et écriture automatique* (José Corti, 1938). See also Cazaux's article "Révolte et docilité dans l'invention poétique surréaliste," *Minotaure* 11 (15 May 1938):27–28.

6. Henri Ey, "La Psychiatrie devant le surréalisme," as quoted by Gaston Ferdière, "Surréalisme et aliénation mentale," in Ferdinand Alquié, ed., *Entretiens sur le surréalisme* (Mouton, 1968), pp. 305 and 306.

7. André Breton, "L'Art des fous, la clé des champs," reprinted in his *Le Surréalisme et la peinture*, definitive edition (Gallimard: 1965), p. 316.

8. See Theodor Spoerri, "L'Armoire d'Adolph Wölfli," *Le Surréalisme, même* 4 (Spring 1958):50, note.

CHAPTER 3—HYSTERIA AND POETRY

1. For some inexplicable reason, Richard Howard in his translation of *Nadja* (New York: Grove Press; London: Evergreen Books, 1960, p. 153), renders "Quelle épreuve pour l'amour, en effet" as "What a test of life, indeed," thus making the succeeding sentence incomprehensible. This, incidentally, is only one of a number of gross errors in Howard's translation that render his version of Breton's book—the only one available in English—totally unreliable.

2. André Breton and Louis Aragon, "Le Cinquantenaire de l'hystérie," *La Révolution surréaliste* 11 (15 March 1928):22. Aragon and Breton were celebrating the fiftieth anniversary of Charcot's experiments with hysterical patients. Their admiration for Charcot's work at the Salpêtrière is not shared by clinicians like David Stafford-Smith, who has observed soberly, "despite the greatness of Charcot as a physician it seems now indisputable that the effect of his work with suggestible patients at these demonstrations was almost without exception to make them worse" [*Psychiatry To-day* (Harmondsworth: Penguin Books, 1952), p. 47]. Still, there is a notable consistency about the surrealists' unshakeable respect for Charcot. His view that hypnosis is a pathological entity and that the capacity to be hypnotized is a sign of abnormality led Charcot to use hypnosis in demonstrations of manifestations of hysteria, but not to treat the disorder. By abstaining from trying to cure hysteria, he endeared himself to the early surrealists in a way that Sigmund Freud could never do.

3. André Breton, "La Médecine mentale devant le surréalisme," *Le Surréalisme au service de la Révolution* 2 (October 1930):31. This essay was inspired by a polemic provoked by *Nadja*. The opinions expressed by Dr. Claude [director of the Sainte-Anne asylum, attacked in *Nadja* (pp. 128–29)] and Dr. Janet were reproduced from the *Annales Médico-psychologiques: journal de l'aliénation mentale et de la médecine légale des aliénés* 12th Ser. 11 (November 1929) at the beginning of Breton's *Second Manifeste du surréalisme* in 1930.

4. Franklin Rosemont, "The 100th Anniversary of Hysteria," preface to the catalogue *Surrealism in 1979: 100th Anniversary of Hysteria* (Cedarwood, Wisconsin: Ozaukee Art Center, 1978), p. 4. The exhibition ran between March 5 and April 9.

5. Published in *La Nouvelle Revue Française* and reprinted in André Breton, *Les Pas perdus* (Gallimard, 1924), p. 96.

6. René Crevel, "Notes en vue d'une psycho-dialectique," *Le Surréalisme au service de la Révolution* 5 (May 1933):55. The reprint of Lacan's *De la Psychose paranoïaque dans ses rapports avec la personnalité* (Editions du Seuil, 1975) is followed by his "Premiers écrits sur la paranoïa," both originally published in a magazine where surrealist influence was significant—*Minotaure*. These writings date from 1933: "Le Problème du style et la conception psychiatrique des formes paranoïaques de l'existence" and "Motifs du crime paranoïaque: le crime des sœurs Papin." Also included in the volume is "Ecrits inspirés: Schizographie," signed by three psychiatrists, Lacan, Lévy-Valensi, and Migault, taken from *Annales Médico-psychologiques* 5 (December 1931). This text deals with automatic writing.

7. Crevel, whose private papers include notes on his readings from Freud, C. G. Jung, and Otto Rank, contributed to the special number of *Le Disque vert* (1924) on Freud and psychoanalysis an article entitled "Freud, de l'alchimiste à l'hygiéniste." There he discussed Freud's therapeutics as a "veritable pastiche." Broadening his remarks, he went on, "And then, if psychoanalysis were to guarantee us a hope of complete human revelation—we should have to think of blowing up the old globe in which only a little mystery induces us to find the hours beautiful, women desirable and men worthy of our friendship."

The ultimate threat of successful therapy—elimination of mystery—prompted Crevel to ridicule psychoanalysis in his novel *Etes-vous fous?* (1929), where the main character suffers from an "anti-Oedipus simplex." The title of an essay, "Des très dérisoires thérapeutiques individuelles," in Crevel's *Le Clavecin de Diderot* (1932) speaks for itself. Here we read, by the way, "In the event that remedies momentarily appear efficacious, there is nothing more precarious than that cure, so long as living conditions and social relationships continue to be those that gave rise to the sick person's sickness, the sick person's crime." However, *Le Clavecin de Diderot* deals seriously with a condition that Crevel calls the Orestes complex. It also offers a ferocious Freudian analysis called "Jésus (Famille et complexes, famille de complexe. Complexe de famille)."

Like Michel Leiris, upon whose autobiography, *L'Age d'homme* (1938), it left an indelible mark, René Crevel underwent psychoanalysis and gladly drew upon its methods in his writings.

8. Reading in the *Petite Gironde* the results of the admission examination to Saint-Cyr, France's West Point, Jean Caupenne and the surrealist Georges Sadoul wrote on August 16, 1929 to the individual who had placed first in the competition. They offered to spank him in public if he did not withdraw from the military academy, pouring contempt upon him and the French army, assuring him, for good measure, "we spit on the three

colors, blue, white and red of the flag you defend." Caupenne subsequently apologized, pleading intoxication as his excuse. As for Sadoul, he was condemned to a fine and a three-month prison term. See *Le Surréalisme au service de la Révolution* 1 (July 1930): 34–40, for details. Commenting on the incident in his *Entretiens*, André Breton would call it a manifestation of black humor, sternly judging it "the most debatable example, in many respects" (p. 163).

CHAPTER 4—"CONSIDERATIONS OF MENTAL HYGIENE"

1. Gaston Ferdière, "Surréalisme et aliénation mentale," in Ferdinand Alquié, ed., *Entretiens sur le surrealisme* (Mouton, 1968), p. 304. On the same occasion Ferdière saluted André Breton as "an escapee from psychiatry" (p. 312).

2. Pierre Mabille, *Thérèse de Lisieux* (1937) (Le Sagittaire, 1975), p. 92. All subsequent parenthetical page references are to the 1975 edition.

3. Radovan Ivsic, "Eternel Voleur des énergies...," postface to the 1975 edition of *Thérèse de Lisieux*, p. 97.

4. Salvador Dalí, "Intellectuels castillans et catelans—expositions—arrestation d'un exhibitionniste dans le Métro," *Le Surréalisme au service de la Révolution* 2 (October 1930):9.

5. Salvador Dalí, "Objets surréalistes," *Le Surréalisme au service de la Révolution* 3 (December 1931):16.

6. From an unsigned article, "War against the Pope," *Arsenal: Surrealist Subversion* 2 (Summer 1973):20. On the same page appears a "Letter from the Surrealists to Benjamín Mendoza y Amor," written by Stephen Schwartz and approved, with due gravity, by all the current adherents to the Surrealist Movement in the United States.

7. The eighth number of *La Révolution surréaliste* (1 December 1926) carries (p. 13) a photograph captioned, "Our associate Benjamin Péret insulting a priest." In a questionnaire for the *Nouveau Dictionnaire des contemporains* completed in Péret's handwriting, we read under the heading "Amusements and Hobbies," the words "insulting priests," while the entry headed "Peculiarities" runs, "detests priests, cops, Stalinists and tradespeople." Péret was a Trotskyist, expelled from Brazil for political activism in 1931 and imprisoned by the French authorities for the same crime after he was recalled to military service in 1940.

8. René Crevel, "The Period of Sleeping Fits," *This Quarter* (September 1932), reprinted in "Surrealism in the service of Revolution," a special number of *Radical America* (January 1970) at p. 18.

9. Francis Gérard, "L'Etat d'un surréaliste," *La Révolution surréaliste* 1 (December 1924):29.

10. Michel Carrouges, *André Breton et les données fondamentales du surréalisme* (Gallimard, 1950), p. 127.

11. Interview printed in André Breton, *Perspective cavalière* (Gallimard, 1970), p. 170.

12. This interview took place on September 23, 1959, and appeared in *La Tour de feu* (Nos. 63–64) in December. It is reprinted in Breton's *Perspective cavalière*.

13. Antonin Artaud, *Van Gogh, le suicidé de la société* (1947) in his *Œuvres complètes* (Gallimard, 1971),13:17.

14. André Breton, *Point du jour* (Gallimard, 1934), p. 240.

15. After his exclusion from the surrealist group, Dalí would reverse himself, pointing up, now, the "rivalry" between the paranoiac-critical method and total automatism. See his preface to René Crevel, *La Mort difficile* (1926), reprinted by Jean-Jacques Pauvert in 1974, p. 9.

CHAPTER 5—HALLUCINATION: INVOLUNTARY AND VOLUNTARY

1. Paul Eluard, "Le Miroir de Baudelaire," reprinted in his *Donner à voir* (Gallimard, 1939), p. 110.

2. Paul Eluard, "Physique de la poésie," reprinted in ibid., p. 74.

3. André Breton, *Point du jour*, p. 56. The text in question, *Légitime Défense*, dated September 1926, originally appeared under the imprint Editions surréalistes in 1926.

4. Benjamin Péret, "La Poésie est UNE et indivisible," *VVV* 4 (February 1944):10.

5. Jules Monnerot, *La Poésie moderne et le sacré* (Gallimard, 1945), p. 50. The phrase rendered here by "directed thought" was borrowed by Tristan Tzara ["Essai sur la situation de la poésie," *Le Surréalisme au service de la Révolution* 4 (December 1931):18] from the French translation, *Métamorphoses et symboles de la libido*, of a work by Jung.

6. Gilles Ehrmann, *Les Inspirés et leurs demeures* [Le Temps, n.d. (1962)], pp. xi–xix.

7. Philippe Soupault, *Profils perdus* (Mercure de France, 1963), p. 166.

8. Pierre Janet, *L'Automatisme psychologique* [Alcan (1889) 1903], p. 477.

CHAPTER 6—INSANITY'S POETIC SIMULATION

1. Louis Aragon, "Le surréalisme et le devenir révolutionnaire," *Le Surréalisme au service de la Révolution* 3 (December 1931):3.

2. André Breton, René Char, Paul Eluard, *Ralentir Travaux* (1930) (José Corti, 1968), p. 13.

3. André Breton and Paul Eluard, *L'Immaculée Conception* (1930) (Pierre Seghers, 1961), p. 83. All subsequent parenthetical page references are to this edition.

4. A Rauzy, "A Propos de l'*Immaculée Conception* d'André Breton et Paul Eluard. Contribution à l'étude des rapports du surréalisme et de la psychiatrie" (thesis for the doctorate in Medicine, Faculty of Medicine, Paris, 1970).

CHAPTER 7—POSSESSION

1. A first sampling of Leiris' glossary appeared in the third number of *La Révolution surréaliste* (15 April 1925), above a note in which Antonin Artaud railed against reason: "Yes here now is the only use to which language can be put henceforth, a means for madness, for eliminating thought, for making a break, the maze of unreason, and not a DICTIONARY in which certain ill-bred pedants from around the Seine [the French Academy] canalize their spiritual shrinkage" (p. 7). On the same page Leiris' own com-

ments include the following: "Dissecting the words we love, without bothering to follow either etymology or agreed signification, we discover their most hidden virtues and the secret ramifications that spread throughout all language, canalized by associations of sound, form and idea. Then language is transformed into an oracle and we have here (however slender it may be) a thread to guide us through the Babel of our minds." The series of texts begun by Leiris under the title "Glossaire: j'y serre mes gloses" finally was published as *Bagatelles végétales* (Jean Aubier, 1956).

2. André Breton, "Braise au trépied de Keridwen," preface to Jean Markale, *Les Grands Bardes gallois* (G. Fall, 1956).

3. The first description of the game called *récits parallèles* appeared in November of 1970 over the signature of Micheline Bounoure, in the first issue of the *Bulletin de liaison surréaliste*—an information bulletin circulated among surrealists and not available to the general public. Further discussion appeared in the second issue (April 1971), where examples were reproduced (pp. 10–14). Still more comments, drawn from an exchange of letters between Vincent Bounoure and Guy Cabanel, are featured in N°. 9 (December 1974):12–15. Examples of *récits parallèles* in English translation are offered in J. H. Matthews, *The Custom-House of Desire* (Berkeley: University of California Press, 1975), pp. 304–12.

4. The only gloss applicable here offers little appeal to reason. In their "Notes sur la poésie," Breton and Eluard comment, "What pride in writing, without knowing what language, verb, comparisons, changes of ideas and tone are; without conceiving the *structure* of the duration of the work, the conditions of its aims; without knowing at all the why, the how! To go green, blue, white from being the parrot . . ." (p. 54).

5. Georges Hugnet, "In the Light of Surrealism," in Alfred J. Barr, Jr., *Fantastic Art, Dada, Surrealism*, 3rd ed. [New York: Museum of Modern Art, (1936), 1947], p. 46.

6. Simon Hantaï and Jean Schuster, "Une Démolition au platane," *Médium: communication surréaliste*, Nouvelle Série, 4 (January 1955):58.

7. Conroy Maddox, "The Exhibitionist's Overcoat," *New Road*, special issue on surrealism, 1943.

8. André Breton and Jean Schuster, "Art poétique," *BIEF: jonction surréaliste* 7 (1 June 1959), no pagination.

9. André Breton, "Signe ascendant," a text dated December 30, 1947, reprinted in his *La Clé des champs* (Les Editions du Sagittaire, 1951), pp. 112–15.

10. An example of writing by the mentally disturbed of a kind it is surprising that the surrealists never cite is the following, by a twenty-five-year-old mother of two, suffering from cyclical psychosis:

> . . . Je près-hume que ce n'est pas ma grand-mère qui est le père, ni la bonne mais le ceintre-esprit. Puis-je conter sur vos fontes et vos Sèvres dans un délaye rapide ou doigt-je fer couvrir mon front quasiment virginal par La os et dard con jugal.
>
> Cher Merdessein.
>
> Est-ce que j'ai une tu meurs?
>
> Si vous pouvez savoir à chaque instant exactement ce que je panse, Recevez tous mes vœux de bonne continuation pour vos vacances et trois timbrées pour la raieponce. Respectueuses poncées.

Quoted by Adolfo Fernandez Zoïla, in *L'Evolution psychiatrique* 44 no. 1 (January–March 1979):36.

11. Philippe Audoin, *Breton* (Gallimard, 1970), p. 198.

12. In this connection see the letter written by Breton on November 5, 1957 to Jean Gaulmier, reproduced in the latter's edition of *Ode à Charles Fourier* (Librairie C. Klincksiek, 1961), pp. 7–8.

CHAPTER 8—GAME PLAYING

1. See Gaston Ferdière, "Surréalisme et aliénation mentale," in Ferdinand Alquié, ed., *Entretiens sur le surréalisme* (Mouton, 1968), p. 309.

2. The special features of the research on which Eluard was reporting in *Le Surréalisme au service de la Révolution* require separate discussion in Chapter 9 below.

3. See *Le Surréalisme au service de la Révolution* 6 (May 1933):19.

4. André Breton, untitled introduction to *L'Un dans l'autre* (Eric Losfeld, 1970), p. 7.

5. Philippe Audoin, "Jeux surréalistes," entry on surrealist games in René Alleau, ed., *Dictionnaire des Jeux* (Tchou, 1964), p. 478.

6. See *Le Surréalisme au service de la Révolution* 6 (May 1933):24.

CONCLUSION

1. The photographs in question are among the six plates borrowed from the second volume of Bourneville and Régnard's *Iconographie photographique de la Salpêtrière*, showing the patient identified as X. L. Augustine in attitudes captioned "Appel," "Erotisme," "Extase," "Moquerie," "Cri," and "Contracture." See A. Gorceix, M. Glisseliger, K. Koin, "Les cinquante ans du cinquantenaire," *Annales Médico-psychologiques* 134, no. 4 (April 1978).

2. Comment made during the discussion following Gaston Ferdière's paper, "Surréalisme et aliénation mentale," in Ferdinand Alquié, ed., *Entretiens sur le surréalisme* (Mouton, 1968), p. 321.

3. On this aspect of surrealist writing see J. H. Matthews, "Grammar, prosody, and French surrealist poetry," *Dada/Surrealism* 9 (1979):83–97.

4. Anne Tholose, "Silence et communication," *L'Evolution psychiatrique* 44, no. 1 (January–March 1979):110.

5. Man Ray quotes Atget as saying, "Don't put my name on it," when referring to one of the photographs used by the surrealists. See Paul Hill and Tom Cooper, "Man Ray," *Camera* (February 1975):40.

6. John Fuller, "Atget and Man Ray in the Context of Surrealism," *Art Journal* 35, no. 2 (Winter 1976–77):132.

7. Quoted by Hill and Cooper, "Man Ray," *Camera* (February 1975):50.

8. Quoted in Minor White, "Atget," *Image* (April 1956): 76.

9. See J. H. Matthews, *Toward the Poetics of Surrealism* (Syracuse: Syracuse University Press, 1976), pp. 9–47.

Index